BEYOND SEX AND ROMANCE?

THE POLITICS OF CONTEMPORARY LESBIAN FICTION

ELAINE HUTTON, EDITOR

First published by The Women's Press Ltd, 1998
A member of the Namara Group
34 Great Sutton Street, London EC1V 0DX

British Library Cataloguing-in-Publication Data
A catalogue record for this book is available from the British Library.

ISBN 0 7043 4537 4

Typeset in Trump Medaeval & Base by FSH Ltd, London.
Printed and bound in Great Britain by Cox & Wyman Ltd,
Reading, Berkshire.

Elaine Hutton has taught English Literature and Women's Writing, and has been a member of lesbian writing groups. She has an MA in English and American Literature of the Twentieth Century. She has worked in a women's centre, with pensioners, and for the youth service, and more recently has been teaching literature and access courses for women. She contributed a chapter on representations of lesbians in popular culture and fiction to the acclaimed book, *All the Rage: Reasserting Radical Lesbian Feminism* (The Women's Press, 1996), and continues to be an active feminist campaigner.

CONTENTS

ACKNOWLEDGEMENTS

Many thanks to all the contributors to this book, for their generosity and patience, for the many discussions during the process, and for their chapters!

To Anira Rowanchild for thinking of the subtitle.

And to Helen Windrath at The Women's Press, for her thorough and careful suggestions and encouragement.

INTRODUCTION

The brutish woman lived in a cave: her hair was unkempt, her legs were hairy, and her teeth were large and strong and yellowish. She hunted for herself, and spent her spare time drawing and painting... Then one day she fell in love. It may not have been love, perhaps it was lust, or perhaps friendship. Whatever the exact nature of the relationship, she worked furiously. In the course of her life she drew hundreds of sketches of the other cave-woman. In time, both of them died... By now, it is firmly established that this woman never was, that she never painted, and never lived.

Suniti Namjoshi, *Feminist Fables*, p63

In the last three decades, representations of lesbians in fiction have proliferated, since the explosion in feminist printing and publishing as a result of the women's movement. In the 1970s, through the writing groups, news-letters, magazines and women's presses that developed, lesbians began to gain a loud and at times angry voice. We could not wait to commit our words to paper. The urgency came as a result of the silencing of our very existence – the lies, the distortions but above all the erasing – as Suniti Namjoshi's opening extract illustrates. The lesbian writing of this time tended to be very much a part of the feminist voice of women's liberation, another means, along with conferences, theory and political action, of challenging male supremacy and imagining a new world in which oppressive structures had been overcome. Thirty years on, it is timely to explore the current state of this writing, as a substantial body of work now exists.

Literature as a way of reflecting and explaining our lives, and, at an even more basic level, writing ourselves into existence, has always been important to lesbians. The contributors to this book acknowledge the importance of lesbian literature as a means to the construction of a conscious political identity, and a number of them talk eloquently of the excitement of initially discovering particular novels which foregrounded lesbian existence, normalised it, suggested it was an enticing option, or, more specifically, centralised black lesbian characters or made lesbian mothers visible. All the novels mentioned in this context went some way towards overturning the negative and hostile representations of lesbians so common elsewhere.

A feature of lesbian fiction from the 1970s onwards, concurrent with the predominant ideology within the women's movement proclaiming that any woman could choose to be a lesbian, were the number of 'coming-out' stories published.[1] A popular novel of this period, Nancy Toder's *Choices* (1980), debated the concept of choice, questioning the dominant belief of biological determinism, that lesbians were 'born that way'. (This ideology made a regrettable comeback in the reactionary 1990s.) Coming-out stories were frequently linked to feminism, as it was seen as a strike against the patriarchy to withdraw from men and give one's sexual and emotional allegiance to women.

This is not to imply that there was not a body of lesbian fiction in existence before the 1970s. However, a lot of this previous fiction had either reflected the hostile essentialist view of lesbians as poor sad creatures who could not help their deviant and perverted predilections – the classic example being Stephen Gordon in *The Well of Loneliness* (Hall, 1928) – or constructed lesbianism as primarily a sexual identity, as the 'pulp' American paperbacks of the

1950s and 1960s demonstrate. It is important to note, though, that writers of these lesbian romances, such as Ann Bannon and Valerie Taylor, often created strong lesbian characters, sometimes with feminist attitudes, as some critics have emphasised. These novelists, writing before second-wave feminism, have been seen as radical for their time. Writing from within the repression of post-war McCarthyism, suburban conformity and limited economic options for women, they managed to create characters fighting for autonomy and the right to express their own sexuality.[2]

Indeed, several contributors to this collection have pointed out that pre-feminist writing can sometimes be more radical than later examples of lesbian fiction (Harne on Highsmith's *The Price of Salt*) or can provide a model and tradition for later writers to build upon (Rowanchild on Maureen Duffy). Some of the writing may also be remarkable for its time in presenting lesbian relationships as accepted and ordinary (Whitelaw on Sarton's *The Small Room*). In the context of acknowledging a debt to the past, Miller, in tracing the tradition of utopian writing, finds a link between first- and second-wave feminism, as Charlotte Perkins Gilman's *Herland* prefigured utopian writing of the 1970s and 1980s.

In considering the position of contemporary lesbian fiction, the title of this collection, *Beyond Sex and Romance?*, poses a political question. Ultimately, how important are sexual identity and romantic love in our representations of ourselves? Have we moved *beyond* the early coming-out stories of the 1970s and 1980s, or the pulp fiction of the 1950s and 1960s, in which girl meets girl, girl beds girl (or girls bed each other) and they disappear into soft focus? Has feminism transformed lesbian literature permanently so that it maintains a radical vision for changing the world? How does the fiction deal with oppressive structures in society? Has it perpetrated negative stereotypes of lesbians as sex-crazed or doomed creatures or contributed to altering the social perceptions of lesbianism?

Whether we have moved beyond sex and romance, or, importantly, whether we *want* to, is a matter for lively debate, as different ideologies have battled for dominance since the mid-1980s. Because of the current diversifying of discourses about what it means to be a lesbian, it is a particularly interesting moment to review contemporary lesbian literature in that, as well as celebrating our literary achievements, it is worth assessing how, in this period, changing values both within lesbian culture and in the wider society have been reflected in lesbian novels.

This book set itself the task of creating an overview of some of the ideological standpoints present in contemporary lesbian fiction, in the hope of beginning to answer the above questions, and stimulating debate about lesbian fiction. It is not claiming to be comprehensive in the authors considered, although there is a broad cross-section, encompassing those who write primarily for a lesbian audience and those who have achieved mainstream recognition, 'literary' writers and popular ones, old and young. There is less variety in terms of race, which may reflect the difficulty, even now, that black lesbian writers have in getting published and recognised, although there is some discussion of racism in lesbian fiction.

The contributors to *Beyond Sex and Romance?* responded very personally to requests for chapters, in terms of who they chose to write about and how they approached the task of exploring the impact of various political discourses on lesbian fiction. Some, like Lis Whitelaw and Jill Radford, decided to write about novelists whose work they really enjoy. Whitelaw's fascinating study of May Sarton raises the question of how lesbians have been viewed for much of the twentieth century, since Sarton wrote novels over a fifty-year period. In her comprehensive survey of Val McDermid's crime novels, Radford has humorously provided some clues as to why activists like to relax with lesbian detective fiction. Both of these contributors engage with the vital question of how lesbian novelists write for mainstream readers, as both Sarton and McDermid consciously do so from very different starting points. The implications of lesbian writers being published by mainstream houses are considered by Vada Hart and Rachel Wingfield. Hart raises the crucial issue of humour as a literary strategy, taking a provocative look at its impact on representations of lesbians in the work of Lisa Alther. Wingfield discusses the meaning of lesbian feminist writing, as well as looking at portrayals of lesbian relationships, through a comparison of three novelists who have received public attention, Sara Maitland, Jeanette Winterson and Emma Donoghue. In reclaiming the term 'zero tolerance' from the political parties who have appropriated it from feminists, Elaine Miller takes a fresh look at utopian and dystopian fiction and its relationship with political activism. She too suggests challenging definitions of lesbian writing.

Anita Naoko Pilgrim, in considering characterisation in terms of race, offers a pertinent analysis to explain why white lesbian writers, while attempting to be anti-racist, nevertheless often represent black characters as peripheral, for example by tokenising them. While exploring instances of convincing characterisation of black people, she draws out suggestions for how representations by white writers could become less artificial in the future. Lynne Harne questions whether lesbian romance is radical lesbian writing. In a controversial critique of the politics of lesbian relationships, she problematises the concept of coupledom, while at the same time discussing representations of lesbian friendships in different contexts.

Anira Rowanchild discusses political writing through a comparison of two writers, one of whom, Maureen Duffy, is accepted as part of the literary hierarchy, while the other, Caeia March, is strongly identified with feminism and the women's movement. By an incisive consideration of how their ideological positions are expressed in their work, her chapter becomes an exploration of political writing in general and the dilemmas which confront any lesbian writer when she attempts a political novel. My own chapter seeks to trace a tradition within lesbian detective fiction, discussing whether the genre has continued to flourish from its radical subversive roots. It surveys hardy perennials like Mary Wings and Sarah Dreher, whilst cultivating Ellen Hart, Maggie Kelly and Manda Scott.

Although contributors took different approaches, common themes and preoccupations emerge. Underlying all the chapters is the question of lesbian identity and how it is defined – for example, through sexual preference and sexual practice, or romantic love, through political activism or, in a time of increased visibility, through lifestyle. Equally important is the question of lesbian writing, and what it is exactly. Is it writing by lesbians, about lesbians? Is it a point of view, or an imaginative vision? A question which recurred as a strand through a number of chapters was how lesbians get on with each other and how this is represented in our fiction. Finally, most of the chapters have a sense of historical perspective, even within a thirty-year span – looking at how lesbian writing has changed and developed over the three decades under discussion, whether and how it reflects the changes in our cultural and political life and the broader society, whether it attempts to create new realities.

Now, at the turn of the century, we need to consider the future of lesbian writing and how it is likely to develop. We want to continue to break the silence that has written us out of history, and nurture and develop our writing. At the same time, as this writing inevitably transmits certain values, it is important to ask *what* values are being transmitted, and whose interests they serve. The contributors to this volume both applaud the achievements of lesbian fiction and scrutinise it critically. They ask to what extent it has continued to challenge prevalent ideologies, and whether it has changed so that it merely perpetuates them. Some choose to highlight what they consider the positive qualities of lesbian writing, while others question particular aspects in order to generate debate about future directions.

Finally, how does lesbian writing address our needs and fulfil our expectations? In taking account of the trends of the past decade or so, is lesbian fiction at the end of the

1990s a literature of resistance or a literature of assimilation into mainstream culture? Book reviews nowadays sometimes praise lesbian authors by saying they write about characters who happen to be gay rather than setting out to write lesbian stories. When considering the future development of our fiction, do we still want lesbian stories, and if so, what are they? And is there a danger, if we assimilate, that, like the cave-woman, we will disappear . . . again?

Elaine Hutton

REFERENCES

Hall, Radclyffe (1928), *The Well of Loneliness*, Virago, London, 1981 edn

Namjoshi, Suniti, *Feminist Fables*, Sheba Feminist Publishers, London, 1981

Toder, Nancy, *Choices*, Persephone Press, Watertown, Massachusetts, 1980

Uszkurat, Carol Ann, 'Mid Twentieth Century Lesbian Romance: Reception and Redress' in Gabriele Griffin, ed, *Outwrite: Lesbianism and Popular Culture*, Pluto Press, London; Boulder, Colorado, 1993

Weir, Angela and Elizabeth Wilson, 'The Greyhound Bus Station in the Evolution of Lesbian Popular Culture' in Sally Munt, ed, *New Lesbian Criticism*, Harvester Wheatsheaf, London, 1992

Wolt, Irene (1995), 'An Interview with Valerie Taylor', *The Lesbian Review of Books*, IV, 3 (Spring 1998)

Zimmerman, Bonnie (1990), *The Safe Sea of Women: Lesbian Fiction 1969–1989*, Onlywomen Press, London, 1992 edn

NOTES

1 For example, Julia Penelope Stanley and Susan J. Wolfe, *The Coming Out Stories*, Persephone Press, Watertown, Massachusetts, 1980.
2 See Weir and Wilson, pp95–111, Uszkurat, pp26–47 and Wolt, p3.

THE EDUCATION OF MAY SARTON: LOVE BETWEEN WOMEN IN FOUR NOVELS BY MAY SARTON

Lis Whitelaw

May Sarton (1912–95) was a poet, novelist and writer of journals. Following the publication of *The Single Hound* in 1938, she wrote eighteen novels, most of which are concerned with the familiar subject matter of fiction: relationships between friends, spouses, lovers, parents and children. They deal almost exclusively with white, middle-class, East Coast Americans – the world in which Sarton spent the greater part of her life.

In this chapter I intend to trace the development of Sarton's treatment of love between women in certain novels, with particular reference to *The Small Room* (1961), *Mrs Stevens hears the mermaids singing* (1965), *A Reckoning* (1978) and *The Education of Harriet Hatfield* (1989). I will also refer to other novels as part of this discussion. Sarton's fiction was written over a period of fifty years, so it is hardly surprising to find that her attitudes change and develop. In these four works in particular it is possible to trace a clear shift in her thinking about women's relationships and to relate this to changing attitudes in society as a direct result of the rise of the women's and gay liberation movements. The later work in particular reveals some quite radical ideas which, as Sarton's journals show, were the result of her own growing politicisation. In considering *The Small Room* and *Mrs Stevens*, it is important to keep in mind their historical context. Written before the second wave of feminism, they have no political analysis and reflect views of lesbianism widely held at the time, but when I first encountered them in the 1970s I read them with delight for the fact that they had interesting, challenging lesbian characters and explored areas of lesbian experience which no other novelist had even touched on.

Sarton was wary of being identified as a specifically lesbian writer. Like other lesbian writers of her generation, she was afraid that it would diminish her status as an artist if she was seen primarily as a 'homosexual' writer: 'Anything homosexual will be taken by the homosexual magazines whether it's good or not. And so much is badly written, self-indulgent. The anger is all right but it should be expressed in a literary way' (Cruikshank, p121). For a long time she fought shy of lesbian subject matter, because, as she wrote in a discussion of *Mrs Stevens* in *Journal of a Solitude* (1973), 'The danger is that if you are placed in a sexual context people will read your work from a distorting angle of vision. I did not write *Mrs Stevens* until I had written several novels concerned with marriage and with family life' (p91).

Despite her reservations, Sarton did feel that she had a 'great responsibility' to write about lesbianism, since she had no family and no regular job and she could therefore 'afford to be honest'. Her desire to avoid being labelled, however, which persisted throughout her life, meant that she never wrote for a specifically lesbian audience. She was remarkable as a writer who elicited very direct and personal responses from readers, many of whom corresponded with her, but, she noted, 'Five percent or less of the letters I get are from Lesbians. The greatest number are from married women with children' (*Recovering* [1980], p81). The number of lesbian readers may have increased somewhat later in her life, but the study of Sarton's audience by Carol Virginia Pohli suggests that her readership remained largely heterosexual. There is clear evidence too that Sarton wrote about lesbian experience, including her own, with an eye to explaining it to these readers. Indeed, in an interview in 1983 she said, 'I see myself as a bridge between the homosexual world and the heterosexual world' (Cruikshank, p121), and she reiterates this idea in her journals for the rest of her life. Her commitment to explaining lesbians to the straight world may be the reason why, in her earlier works *The Small Room* and *Mrs Stevens*, she does little to challenge stereotypical ideas about lesbians, presenting their lives as full of pain and basically unfulfilled. It is only later, presumably as a result of her own greater political awareness in the 1970s, and that of her audience, that she chooses to write about love between women in a spirit of celebration.

In her journal *Recovering*, which covers the years 1978 and 1979, she wrote, '[I] wonder whether I am after all evading a real responsibility, to write, as so many people ask me, a novel about women in love. I feel great resistance to the idea' (p90). In fact she never wrote a novel in which a successful domestic relationship between women is the focus in the way that heterosexual marriage is the focus in, for example, *Birth of a Grandfather* (1957) or *Kinds of Love* (1970). Instead she explores the limitations of relationships in *The Small Room* and *Mrs Stevens*, while in *A Reckoning* the central lesbian relationship is neither domestic nor sexual. In *Harriet Hatfield* the protagonist engages with the lives of a community of women after a long-term relationship which, she comes to realise, has restricted rather than liberated her. While in the two earlier novels it is possible to see the depiction of the relationships as reinforcing stereotypical and essentially negative perceptions of lesbian experience, her resistance to writing a novel which concentrated on 'women in love' may, paradoxically, have freed her to write about a far greater variety of women's relationships in her later work in which the relationships, and Sarton's attitude to them, are both positive and radical.

Although there are significant differences in the way Sarton represents lesbian relationships in her novels, all the works share a concern with the conflict between solitude and sharing. This is a conflict which has been much discussed in writing about women and creativity from Virginia Woolf's *A Room of One's Own* onwards. Both in her fiction and in the exploration of her own life in her journals, May Sarton has repeatedly suggested that it is not any easier to combine the two simply because one's partner is a woman. All her protagonists are women with serious lives and aspirations, and her depiction of them makes very clear Sarton's own belief that intimate relationships restrict autonomy and can destroy creativity. The evidence of her journals is that this view derives very much from her own experience, but it is interesting to note that this debate about autonomy, so much a feature of radical lesbian discussion in the 1970s, is not reflected in much of the lesbian fiction and indeed non-fiction written in the past twenty years. Coming-out stories and popular lesbian fiction have frequently colluded to present coupledom as the ultimate goal of 'becoming a lesbian'.

Sarton's analysis of relationships can in this respect be seen as quite radical from the time of *The Small Room* onwards, but in other ways this novel reinforces received ideas about the basis of lesbian partnerships and the emotional distress inherent in them. In the novel a young instructor, Lucy Winter, arrives at a women's college in New England and precipitates a crisis when she discovers that a brilliant student and the protégée of the college's star scholar, Carryl Cope, has plagiarised an academic article. Lucy's belief that the student needs psychiatric help embroils her in an argument that divides the faculty. The issue is further complicated by the fact that Olive Hunt, one of the college trustees, will cancel her large bequest if a college psychiatrist is appointed. Olive has been the lover of Carryl for twenty years.

Freudian assumptions about gender and sexuality underlie the novel, so that Carryl can say without irony, 'I have certainly tried to be my own father' (p196), and it is implicit in the portrayal of the two women that while she is 'mannish', Olive is more 'womanly'; she had wanted them to live together while Carryl had resisted. Olive tells Lucy, 'Carryl is like a man of course', adding that her lack of involvement with her students is also masculine behaviour. 'Women,' on the other hand, 'wear each other out with their everlasting touching of the nerve' (p203). As the relationship ends, Carryl tells Lucy, 'Olive used to interrupt me a dozen times a day. The phone sometimes rang every five minutes', adding, 'I, on the other hand, am glad to be rid of it all, to know there will never be another voice pulling me away from one self to another.' Her final word on the twenty-year partnership is, 'I've wasted too much time' (p245).

At this time Sarton subscribed to the commonly held view that homosexual relationships were inherently less stable than heterosexual ones since 'love is never going to fulfil in the usual sense' (*Journal of a Solitude*, p91). In the novel a heterosexual marriage is also put under strain by the row about the student, but in that case the couple are reconciled. The fact that it is the lesbian relationship that founders could be attributed to the lack of self-awareness of the women involved – Lucy sees them as 'powerful and powerfully unconscious' (p82) – but it could also reflect the limitations, as Sarton sees them, of lesbian relationships.

It is hardly surprising that in a novel written in 1961, Sarton does not overthrow the ideas about lesbianism which were then current, and the portrayal of the two women does emphasise the disadvantages rather than the qualities which had enabled the relationship to endure for twenty years. On the other hand, it is important to remember that at the time when the novel was written, the matter-of-fact way in which the relationship is accepted by other members of the college faculty and the unsensational role it plays in the narrative as a whole were in themselves ground-breaking. In a broader context, a novel written in 1961 that celebrates women's autonomous struggle for self-knowledge and intellectual achievement and which depicts the teacher–student relationship as important in women's lives is trying to do something new and original.

May Sarton published *Mrs Stevens hears the mermaids singing* in 1965 and it is important to bear the date of publication in mind when analysing it in lesbian feminist terms. In the novel two young literary journalists, a man and a woman, come to interview the seventy-year-old woman poet Hilary Stevens. During the course of the interview she discusses her life and especially the women who have been the muses for her writing. This central narrative is framed by one dealing with Hilary's friendship with a young man, Mar, who is struggling to come to terms with his own homosexuality. Her solution to his anger and intermittent self-disgust is to encourage him to try writing poetry and to nurture his talent.

For a contemporary lesbian feminist reader, the novel contains much that is rewarding, and yet the representation of Hilary Stevens will often seem far removed from our own experience, even if we too are writers battling with the tension between creativity and intimacy. At this time Sarton still viewed lesbians as aberrant, the more so if they were also artists. The novel certainly broke new ground by being 'about a woman homosexual who is not a sex maniac, a drunkard, a drug-taker or in any way repulsive; [portraying] a homosexual who is neither pitiable nor disgusting, without senti-mentality', but Sarton felt that the account has to 'face the truth that such a life is rarely happy, a life where art must become the primary motivation, for love is never going to fulfil in the usual sense' (*Journal of a Solitude*, p91). And at one point in the novel Mrs Stevens says, 'When the artist is a woman she fulfils [her talent] at the *expense* of herself as a woman' (p191, Sarton's emphasis). Much of the novel seems to be autobiographical and to have its origin in Sarton's attempts to understand the particular pain and difficulty she experienced as a woman poet.

This autobiographical project means that Sarton adheres to a theory of women's creativity which has its basis in a biologically determined view of gender and which ignores earlier ideas of a female literary tradition. This is particularly surprising since in her poem 'My Sisters, O

My Sisters', published in 1948, she looks back to the women writers who have gone before. While she writes of them as 'Strange monsters' who all know, 'Something is lost, strained, unforgiven in the poet', she recognises that they all seek, 'To come to the deep place where poet becomes woman/Where nothing has to be renounced or given over'. And the place they come to is specifically a female one; an option she does not fully offer to Hilary Stevens in the novel.

While the idea of a women's literary tradition has acquired a new strength and depth with the work of critics who came out of the second wave of feminism and were thus publishing after *Mrs Stevens* was written, many earlier women writers, and especially lesbians, have for much of this century sought to locate themselves in relation to other women writers and often in opposition to a male tradition. Even so, Sarton apparently chooses to emphasise the extent to which Mrs Stevens perceives herself as an anomaly, with all the consequent pain, rather than, at the very least, enabling her protagonist to acknowledge that the struggles which she experiences are shared by other women writers.

Hilary Stevens discovers poetry and the love of women as a teenager, but until late in her life she can explain her need for a female muse only in terms of a male persona. As she tells Mar, 'It was (and *is*) the boy in me who wrote the poems' (p217). Although she marries briefly, only women inspire her to write: 'She was sometimes moved to tears just seeing Adrian walk into the room ... but whatever she felt for him it had nothing to do with writing poetry' (p48).

Sarton's open exploration of the idea that a woman poet can draw inspiration from her feelings for women reflects her own liberal attitude to homosexuality. Celebrating the honesty of the Bloomsbury Group about their personal lives, she wrote, 'They accepted that nearly everyone connected with the arts is going to have to come to terms with sexual ambivalence, and to cope with being bisexual, and that passionate friendships may involve sex', and seemed to think at this time that there was no need to differentiate between homosexual and heterosexual relationships: 'There are going to be many and complex relationships that nourish, and many kinds of love' (*Journal of a Solitude*, p150). Her representation of Hilary's feelings for women does, however, seem to endorse her heroine's persistence in seeing lesbian relationships in terms of societally determined gender roles: 'Powerful women may be driven to seek the masculine in each other' (p173).

In the novel, Mrs Stevens has sexual relationships with two women and is inspired by several others, one of whom she never meets. She sleeps with a friend and mentor, Willa, only once and she has a full-scale relationship with Dorothea, a distinguished sociologist. Neither of these consummated relationships has a satisfactory outcome. Willa suffers a stroke after their single transcendent night together and Dorothea and Hilary share a life that is tormented and verbally violent for much of the time. When Dorothea's academic book is a success, Hilary is driven to a violence of rage which destroys the relationship. During their time together Hilary is unable to write. When the two women spend a summer together, Hilary retreats into domesticity, arranging flowers and sewing curtains rather than writing poetry.

Again Sarton returns to her theme of the conflict between creativity and a domestic relationship. 'No partner in a love relationship (whether homosexual or heterosexual) should feel that he [*sic*] has to give up an essential part of himself to make it viable,' she wrote in *Journal of a Solitude*, adding that her own creative activity had been achieved 'at a high price in emotional maturity and unhappiness' (p122). It is perhaps not surprising, if Sarton felt this way, that Hilary has no more partners after Dorothea. She has learned from the experience and come to terms with herself as a woman. But even now she cannot think of herself as a poet in entirely gender-free terms: 'In the end we were each broken in half. The boy in me was dead. I had to go on as a woman ... We were nearly dead; we each knew this was a final relationship. There could be no other. But we had turned the Medusa face around and seen our *selves*. The long solitude ahead would be the richer for it' (p170).

Hilary Stevens seems unable to imagine the possibility of a poet at peace with herself as a woman and, as one might expect of a woman of her generation, her view of gender is firmly biological in its determinism. Sarton explores the theme of the responsibility to one's talent in her auto-biographical writing as well, and the capacity for anger and despair with which she endows Hilary Stevens is almost certainly autobiographical in its origins: 'But the deep collision is and has been with my unregenerate, tormenting and tormented self' (*Journal of a Solitude*, p12). What she denies her fictional protagonist is the possibility of the domestic tranquillity which she herself enjoyed for many years with her long-term partner, Judy Matlack, and came to enjoy again towards the end of her life.

Contemporary readers may well feel that the argument about what it means to be a woman and a writer has moved on since Sarton wrote *Mrs Stevens* and that the emphasis on Hilary's male-identification dates the novel. None the less, this work confronts the perennial conflict between the need for solitude and the need for intimacy with great originality and passion. It is certainly the most autobiographical of Sarton's novels and there is a defiance in her celebration of the 'strange monster' that is the creative woman. The overwhelming impression left by the novel is of the price a woman pays for her talent, but when Hilary Stevens says to Mar at the end of the novel, 'I think I would like to have been a woman, simple and fruitful, a woman with many children, a great husband...and no talent' (p291), the reader does not really believe her. The excitement of being a poet, the rewards of being 'a person of primary intensity', are celebrated too wholeheartedly.

As We Are Now (1973) is a brief and surprising novel which covers the same territory as Sarton's later journals. In these, from *At Seventy* (1984) to her last published work, *At Eighty-Two* (1996), Sarton tells us some of the first stories we have of what it is like to grow old and become ill as an autonomous woman, and specifically as a lesbian. The novel, however, was written while she was only in her early sixties. The spinster heroine of *As We Are Now*, Caro Spencer, is put in an old people's home in the depths of the New England countryside, where she is treated with harshness and at times actual cruelty. The novel is a first-person account of her struggle to maintain her sanity and self-respect in the face of daily assaults upon them by her carers. When, in the absence of the home's owner, she is looked after for a while by a kind local woman, Anna Close, Caro forms a deep attachment to her. Despite the differences in background and education between them, Caro learns about love through her feelings for Anna: 'How very strange that at seventy-six in a relationship with an inarticulate person who cannot put any of it into words, I myself am on the brink of understanding things about love I have never understood before' (p98). But almost at once Caro experiences the limitations as well as the joys of loving another woman. She has come to understand why old men fall in love with their nurses, but, unlike them, 'I cannot offer Anna marriage or take her into my life, or in any way help her as she helps me' (p99). After Anna leaves, Caro writes to her, telling her something of her feelings; the letter is discovered by the staff and they tell her she is 'filthy' to feel this way about another woman. Caro's response to this treatment shows Sarton's growing political awareness as a novelist. Appalled by her treatment, Caro starts by judging herself by the standards of those who condemn her. She accepts that she has 'become a leper' to herself and is afraid to 'contaminate' a young woman who has been visiting her. But she then sees that if she is beyond the pale, 'I have my own ideas of what those beyond the pale do – the blacks for instance. They finally come to see that violence is the only answer to oppression. They make bombs. What was good in them becomes evil. They want only to destroy' (p107). Her response to the treatment she has received is to burn down the home, killing herself and all the other inmates. Sarton's politics remain liberal in their analysis and as yet she does not differentiate between homophobia and other forms of oppression; for Caro and, I think, for Sarton herself, they are all part of the same phenomenon. But the novel is remarkable for its time and remains so. There are not many radical old women in novels written in the early 1970s.

When *A Reckoning* was first published in 1978, one reviewer claimed that it was a 'concealed homosexual novel' (*Recovering*, p67), an accusation which upset May Sarton very much. She was disturbed that she was being accused of cowardice in failing to write openly about homosexuality and was afraid that, if she was labelled as a lesbian writer, her 'power to be useful in liberal causes' would be compromised in the same way that those who had been accused of Communism in the McCarthy era had been compromised: 'The vision of life in my work is not limited to one segment of humanity or another and it has little to do with sexual proclivity. It does have to do with love and love has many forms' (p81).

A Reckoning is certainly a novel about love between women. The central relationship is not sexual but it is the most important attachment in the lives of the two women and there is a lesbian subplot. The novel opens with the main character, Laura, confronting the news that she is dying of lung cancer. She is determined to organise her own death and the novel deals mainly with the way that she presents it to her friends and family, and their various reactions to the news. The person she thinks about most is her old friend Ella, with whom she had been a student in Paris and whom she describes as her 'spiritual twin'. At first, apart from her elderly aunt, Minna, Ella is the only person Laura tells about her illness. As the novel progresses, Laura remembers her life, especially her difficult relationship with her mother, but this is always framed by what she and Ella shared as young women and which Ella writes to her about from her home in England. In her initial letter Laura had told Ella not to come to her, but when she is finally dying Ella arrives unbidden.

'"I couldn't let go,"' Laura explains to her. '"And I didn't know what I was waiting for."' She adds later, '"But I've thought of you, of Paris, of us nearly every day since [the doctor] told me,"' (p249). Laura tells Ella that she feels her journey towards death has been a way of connecting herself to all other women. She has begun to understand that there is 'communion. Something women are only beginning to tap, to understand, a kind of tenderness towards each other as women' (p252). It is clear that these feelings towards women in general spring from her feelings for Ella. Laura asks Ella why they have not been lovers, for she has acknowledged, 'the aura of sensuality, of passion even that had surrounded her and Ella, although it was never played out except in those ravishing kisses they pretended were "quite all right"', and Ella reminds her of the climate of opinion which would have made it hard: 'We had been poisoned by the whole ethos, taught to be mortally afraid of what our bodies tried to teach us...A passionate love would have created terrible conflict...I truly believe we had the best of it' (p14).

This treatment of female friendship is much more feminist than any that Sarton has written before and it explicitly acknowledges the way in which society prevents women exploring their lesbian sexuality fully. It also draws attention to the way in which women are learning to share their experience and value their relationships with each other. Her feelings for Ella have been more important than any others for Laura, including those for her husband and children, and thus I would argue that, despite May Sarton's own opinion, it can be described as a lesbian novel. Adrienne Rich's definition of the 'lesbian continuum' as a range of 'woman-identified experience; not simply the fact that a woman has had or consciously desires genital sexual experience with another woman' (Rich, p20) has been much criticised, not least for the fact that it fails to acknowledge the importance of self-definition in the recognition of a lesbian identity, but it does offer a way of including non-genital relationships of primary intensity within the realm of lesbian experience. Rich's article had not been published by the time *A Reckoning* was written and Sarton herself might have resisted its use as a way to include the novel in the lesbian canon. In any event, the power and importance of women's friendship which the novel celebrates are specifically part of a feminist analysis of relationships and again Sarton is mapping territory barely charted by other novelists.

In both *A Reckoning* and later in *The Education of Harriet Hatfield*, the heroines have close male relatives who are gay. By this device Sarton seems to make a number of points. On one level she suggests the prevalence and perhaps the ordinariness of homosexuality; on another she uses it as a way to show both the shared experience of lesbians and gay men and, especially in *Harriet Hatfield*, the areas where our experience is very different. In both novels there are also other lesbian characters. In *A Reckoning*, Laura, an editor in a publishing house, chooses, despite her illness, to continue to work with a young lesbian writer on publishing her autobiographical novel. Initially the writer, Harriet, wants to publish under a pseudonym because she cannot face coming out to her parents, but later decides that she cannot publish at all because her 'friend', Fern, is terrified of losing her job as a teacher if it is known that she is a lesbian. '"People pay a high price, I think, for leading a life they are not willing to live publicly,"' (p65) observes Laura, but Harriet reminds her forcefully of the dangers. Sarton's treatment here of lesbian experience shows an awareness of more contemporary concerns than she addressed in *Mrs Stevens* and *The Small Room*. When Laura thinks of her sister Jo, who has never come to terms with her feelings for women, she recognises that their mother, Sybille, did her daughter great harm by breaking off Jo's affair with another woman and she tells Harriet that by denying her sexuality Jo has become a 'half-person'. Most importantly, though, Laura feels a commitment to working with Harriet because of her own feelings for Ella.

In this novel one can see quite clearly how Sarton fulfils her self-selected function as 'a bridge between the homosexual world and the heterosexual world'. The question Laura is trying to answer before she dies is, 'What was it then to be a woman?', and she comes up with the answer that it is 'More complex and far more difficult than it is to be a man' (p111). The way that Sarton presents the 'lesbian continuum' in the novel would give heterosexual readers an answer which might seriously challenge some of their preconceptions and Sarton is clear that by deciding to publish, even at the risk of destroying her relationship with Fern, Harriet is behaving honourably, making the kind of sacrifice that is demanded of writers if they are to tell the truth. Laura praises Harriet for the fact that her novel treats lesbianism 'naturally and without sensationalism' (p65) and says that it will help at least a few people to 'understand it all a little better' (p141). This surely is what Sarton herself is aiming to do in *A Reckoning*. It is a tender and lyrical novel and there is nothing cowardly or dishonest in the way in which Sarton portrays the feelings of Laura and Ella, as her hostile critic claimed. In some ways the fact that they are not lovers makes the book more radical rather than less so, but its message may well be more startling to a heterosexual rather than to a lesbian reader.

The Education of Harriet Hatfield is the last of Sarton's novels and deals more explicitly with contemporary lesbian issues than any earlier work. Harriet is sixty and her partner of thirty years, Vicky, has just died, leaving her comfortably off. Throughout their life together Vicky has gone out to work as a publisher, while Harriet has worked at home, tending the house and garden. With Vicky's death she has reached a turning point in her life and she decides to leave her elegant house, cut off from the world by high walls, and open a women's bookstore in Somerville, a working-class suburb of Boston. Harriet has been protected in her relationship with Vicky by her class and affluence and so she is unprepared for the hostility she encounters from the local community. The whole issue of homophobia is to the fore in this novel, as slogans are sprayed on her windows, wood is stolen from her outhouse and she suffers one last attack which finally rallies people to her support. The revelation of all this hatred comes as a shock to Harriet, as does the discovery that the police are 'not about to protect gays' (p246). A young lesbian college professor tells Harriet how she was attacked in the street while taking part in a march for lesbian and gay housing rights and how the police did not regard the two gay men who offered to make statements about it as reliable witnesses because of their sexuality. Through this account and her own experience, Harriet comes to realise that she is 'in the front line of a war you never chose', as her friend Nan puts it. 'Or even knew existed,' Harriet adds (p262). Nan and her husband have moved to Somerville because they did not want to bring up their children in the racist atmosphere of the neighbourhood where they lived before.

The main theme of the book is Harriet's education in what it means to be a lesbian when you are not protected by money or a powerful partner. Through this education, she becomes able to own and be proud of her identity as a lesbian. Initially at the opening of the bookstore she winces when one of the younger customers says, '"You are some brave lesbian"' and admits that she does not like 'that open word' (p31). She explains that Vicky hated it and then adds that she resists labels because it 'seems to create distance rather than intimacy'. The younger lesbian retorts that for her the use of the word is 'a matter of honour' (p32). When two older lesbians who come into the shop warn her about the dangers of homophobia, she shrugs it off, but is nettled when one of them suggests that it is her money which makes her feel safe. Harriet makes it clear that she and Vicky did not have lesbian friends and confides to her straight friend Caroline that she had no idea what other lesbians had to contend with. When Harriet inadvertently 'comes out' in a newspaper interview, her elder brother, Fred, is scandalised, but by this time Harriet recognises that she is in a good position to make a stand: 'If someone with money, who cannot be fired from a job, who has no children, whose lover is dead, comes out it may be one way to change the public mind about that word you can't bring yourself to utter. I said what I did in the hope of building a bridge across all this homophobia' (p110).

As she forges a new identity for herself, Harriet is able to both mourn Vicky's death and reflect on the nature of their relationship. Several other women in the novel, her old friend Caroline, who has been married with children, and Sandra, a friend from her college days, both acknowledge that they have loved women. Another close friend, Angelica, goes so far as to admit that she still feels disturbed by the ambivalent emotions she experienced at college when another young woman fell in love with her. As a result she has been hostile towards Harriet ever since the publication of the interview. In this novel Sarton seems to be charting passionate female friendship in various degrees of intensity and implicitly presenting them all as stages on the 'lesbian continuum' in a way that she could not in *A Reckoning*. In *Harriet Hatfield* Harriet appears to make no distinction between her friends' relationships and hers with Vicky. She acknowledges the sexual side of the relationship and then reflects that what she misses most is 'the tender loving, the physical closeness long after the first passionate year was over' (p152). When Caroline asks her why women love other women, she replies, 'For a woman, another woman is not primarily a sexual object whereas for a man she often *is*. A woman wants to be recognised as a person first, to be understood and cherished for what she *is*, and especially in middle age she may find this kind of understanding and recognition with another woman' (p170). For Harriet, then, sex is not the main issue, although she does admit that she felt intense jealousy when Vicky was unfaithful to her, and her experience leads her to celebrate the other aspects of her relationship with Vicky. When she has spoken to Caroline, however, she feels that her response was inadequate and she admits to herself that one of the charms of a lesbian relationship is 'not having to make allowances for the male compulsions and fundamental sense of superiority' (p171). To a radical reader this may not seem much of an admission, but it is the first time in Sarton's fiction that a character has admitted that it may actually be *preferable* to be a lesbian.

Through her conversations with the numerous lesbians of all ages who come into the shop and through reading the books that she stocks, Harriet comes to new understandings about herself and Vicky. Vicky had always teased Harriet because as a child she had never wanted to wear boy's clothes while Vicky had managed to persuade her mother to let her wear a boy's sailor suit in the summer at a time when such things were unheard of. Harriet now recognises that Vicky's idea of herself was 'old-fashioned': 'Lesbian women today talk about being whole women, not about being imitation men like Radclyffe Hall' (p206). Harriet, sixty in the 1980s, marks a major development in Sarton's fictional representation of lesbians. Hilary Stevens, seventy in the late 1960s, saw her sexuality and creativity in terms of a boy trapped inside a woman: Harriet, with the benefit of feminism and lesbian debates about sexuality, is able to rejoice at the idea of lesbians as 'whole women'.

In the light of her new understanding, Harriet can look back and see that Vicky dominated her, keeping at bay the 'real life' which she has been able to engage with since her partner's death. This 'real life' involves connection with other lesbians, with gay men and with a wider community of women, including the black woman, Nan. The connection is more political than any Sarton has depicted before, as Harriet achieves a sense of self and of freedom by acknowledging 'the kind of loneliness and isolation anyone who deviates from the norm goes through. I am a part of a minority and I never took that in while Vicky was alive, so I understand a lot I never understood till now. Some of it is painful' (p311).

In this, the most political of her novels, Sarton depicts Harriet making common cause not only with lesbians but with gay men: her brother Andrew, who comes out to her after the publication of the interview, and Joe and Eddie, who offer support and physical protection in the early days of the threats against her and whose case she then prepares to fight when they are threatened with eviction because Eddie has AIDS. In this novel Sarton depicts, for the first time in her fiction, lesbian and gay relationships which are subject to the kinds of pressure that her readers will recognise.

Writing movingly of death and bereavement, Sarton deals too with areas rarely explored by younger writers. While the book may not seem radical to women who have been part of feminism and lesbian activism, it reminds us of the enormous changes that have taken place over the past twenty-five years and the way that older lesbians like Harriet, and Sarton herself, have had their ideas challenged. The novel celebrates those who have taken up the challenge and used it as a basis for growth and self-realisation.

The characters in Sarton's fiction represent the changing nature of lesbian identity through much of the twentieth century: from the struggles of Hilary Stevens to be both a woman and a poet, through the mannishness of Carryl Cope, to the activism of Harriet Hatfield, who, like Sarton herself, came to see the political dimension of her sexuality and was freed by it. In parallel with Sarton's own life her characters move from a world where the focus is on individuals and their relationships to a wider sphere of solidarity and feminism where love between women need not be sexual and can act as the motive force for resistance and activism, for creativity and poetry. Like Laura in *A Reckoning*, and like Sarton herself, they are all exploring what it means to be a woman – and a lesbian.

REFERENCES

Works by May Sarton
Sarton, May, *Birth of a Grandfather*, Norton, New York,
    1957
—(1961), *The Small Room*, Norton, New York, 1976 edn;
    The Women's Press, London, 1996
—(1965), *Mrs Stevens hears the mermaids singing*,
    Norton, New York, 1975 edn; The Women's Press,
    London, 1993
—(1968), *Plant Dreaming Deep*, Norton, New York, 1983
    edn; The Women's Press, London, 1995
—, *Kinds of Love*, Norton, New York, 1970 edn; The
    Women's Press, London, 1995
—(1973), *As We Are Now*, The Women's Press, London,
    1983 edn
—, *Journal of a Solitude* (1973), Norton, New York, 1977
    edn; The Women's Press, London, 1985
—(1978), *A Reckoning*, The Women's Press, London,
    1984 edn
—, *Selected Poems*, Serena Sue Hilsinger and Lois
    Brynes, eds, Norton, New York, 1978
—(1980), *Recovering*, Norton, New York, 1986 edn; The
    Women's Press, London, 1997
—, *At Seventy*, Norton, New York, 1984
—(1989), *The Education of Harriet Hatfield*, The
    Women's Press, London 1990 edn
—, *At Eighty-Two*, Norton, New York, 1996; The
    Women's Press, London, 1996

Other References
Cruikshank, Margaret, 'A Conversation with May
    Sarton', in Margaret Cruikshank, ed, *The Lesbian
    Path*, Grey Fox Press, San Francisco, 1985
Pohli, Carol Virginia, 'Saving the Audience: Patterns of
    Reader Response to May Sarton's Work', in Susan
    Swartzlander and Marilyn M. Mumford, eds, *That
    Great Sanity: Critical Essays on May Sarton's Work*,
    University of Michigan Press, Ann Arbor, 1995

Rich, Adrienne, *Compulsory Heterosexuality and Lesbian Existence*, Onlywomen Press, London, 1981

Woolf, Virginia, *A Room of One's Own*, Hogarth Press, London, 1929

THE STATE OF THE HEART: IDEOLOGY AND NARRATIVE STRUCTURE IN THE NOVELS OF MAUREEN DUFFY AND CAEIA MARCH

Anira Rowanchild

At the beginning of *The Microcosm* (1966), Maureen Duffy gives an ironic anthropological account of an obscure and isolated social group. She notes that it is particularly interesting 'that their language has no form of the verb to be nor any way of expressing past or future time. The philosophical concept of existence or being is quite beyond their grasp. Everything simply happens in an eternal present' (pp23–4). The group is an analogy for the microcosmic world of the lesbian. In this chapter I shall examine the attempts by two lesbian writers, Maureen Duffy and Caeia March, to dispel the patriarchal myth that, for lesbians, there is no way of expressing past or future, and no verb to be. I shall compare the ways in which Duffy and March manifest their ideological positions in their writing, and investigate how these affect narrative structure, characterisation and style, and whether their engagement with their readers changes over time.

Duffy is the older of the two writers. She was born in 1933. Her first overtly lesbian novel, *The Microcosm*, came out in 1966. This was twenty years before The Women's Press published March's first novel *Three Ply Yarn*, and still several to go before radical lesbian feminism became a recognisable political phenomenon in the 1970s. Duffy describes in an Afterword to the 1989 Virago edition of *The Microcosm* how she had the idea of writing a non-fiction book, 'a treatment of female homosexuality which would delineate the state of the heart in the early sixties when we were presumably in the middle of a sexual revolution towards a more open society'. No publishing house would accept her proposal because it was 'such a risky subject' and Duffy had no academic qualifications 'in the sociology or psychology of sex'. Instead of giving up the project, Duffy wrote a novel, basing it on the interviews she had taped with a number of lesbians of varying 'age, class, occupation and geographical spread' (p269).

The Microcosm is a dense novel. There are no chapter breaks and each character's story slides into the next without warning. Often conventional punctuation and sentence formation are abandoned. The unity of historical time, the mid-1960s, is suddenly dislocated by the account of the adventures of an eighteenth-century cross-dressing lesbian. (We are now used to characters from another century popping up in contemporary writing – Doll Sneerpiece in Jeanette Winterson's 1995 novel *Art & Lies*, for example – but Duffy was innovating in 1966.) The nearest thing we get to a central character in *The Microcosm* is the butch Matt, who is confusingly referred to throughout the novel by the masculine pronoun.

Duffy undoubtedly set herself a very difficult task, and, in a pub poll of lesbian readers, I found unanimous agreement that *The Microcosm* is 'a difficult book'. While several readers felt they had got a lot out of it, others said they just could not cope with its apparent structurelessness and lack of proper story, or were repelled at once by the butch/femme stereotypes that the opening pages appear to endorse.

The formal structure of the novel *is* demanding. Duffy explains that, rather than composing her characters into the novel's customary linear narrative, she chose to situate them within an earlier tradition of 'myth, saga, romance and fairy tale'. These early fictions more easily allow for digression, inconsequentiality, unexplained events and a rapid shift between voices and styles – devices that help to decentralise the narrative and create perhaps a more appropriately non-patriarchal configuration. Whether Duffy intended her literary experiments as a challenge to male power is not clear. She has said that, in using these earlier forms of fiction, she hoped to subvert the received literary doctrine that the novel was a form developed for the amusement of 'a middle-class female reader with time on her hands' (The Microcosm, p290). But does The Microcosm also have the effect of offering a radical analysis of sexual politics?

One of the problems in identifying the ideological position at the heart of The Microcosm is Matt. She is the only character to have a continuous narrative voice, employing a world-weary authorial tone we guess is Duffy's own: 'Matt has heard it all before and will hear it all again for there is nothing new under the all-seeing eye that can be said on the level of polemics about the problems of minority groups ... that will convince either side since they both speak from their own needs' (p172). Despite her lengthy philosophical monologues and didactic dialogue, Matt never emerges as a concrete figure. Very late in the novel, when she meets an old university colleague and we unexpectedly learn of her past as a promising archaeology student, we get a brief glimpse of a character located in historical time. Otherwise Matt is a shadowy female Prospero, casting her own 'all-seeing eye' over the struggling islanders shipwrecked in the House of Shades, as she calls the London lesbian club that Duffy loosely based on the famous now-defunct Gateways club.

Duffy's use of the male pronoun for Matt, and for a number of other characters, is also distracting, and disturbing to contemporary readers. On one level Duffy may simply be reflecting the actual form of address of her original interviewees, observing a tradition among lesbians who see themselves as butch. However, the persistent use of 'he' and 'him', not only in reported speech but also in passages of narrative, is clearly meant to impress the reader with a sense of the gender ambiguity, and even perhaps the biological difference, of these butch

lesbians. In a discussion about gender roles, Matt opposes
her own way of tackling the difficult questions of personal
identity – arguing, talking round abstractions – to that of
Rae (her lover), whose intuitive response is to 'simply get
on with it'. 'It's the old, the traditional difference, I
suppose between masculine and feminine ways of
approach', Matt says. Matt's use of 'traditional' seems to
imply a cultural origin to gender roles, but one of the
habituées of the House of Shades, Steve (Miss Stephens,
the games mistress), ponders on the different kinds of
lesbian, opposing Matt's 'congenital type', to a psychological model: 'most of us are looking for our mothers'
(p35). *The Microcosm* was written several years before
lesbian feminist consciousness was fully articulated and
Duffy presents without discrimination or authorial
comment a spectrum of ideas about lesbian identity
current in the 1960s.

Although *The Microcosm* sometimes offers a simplistic
version of lesbian existence, in many passages Duffy
shows herself capable of complicating the stereotypes. For
example, the mother of one of Miss Stephens' pupils
experiences a breakdown as a result of recognising, in
Steve's lesbianism, the lost possibilities of her own
sexuality. And even Matt is shown struggling to construct
a sense of self beyond the two-dimensional cultural
stereotypes: 'I am what I have become and will be what I
will be' (p17). Duffy also links that struggle with the
economic pressures on women – 'think of the money she'd
be earning, the jobs she could have had with her
experience if she'd been born a boy' (p201). At the same
time, Duffy's characters refer to themselves as 'inverts'
and seem reconciled to living as negative figures within
the microcosm of the House of Shades. Sheila Jeffreys has
written that 'Duffy chooses to express the sadness of the
lesbian bar scene [in *The Microcosm*]. The positive virtues
of support and friendship and rebelliousness that bars
offered are not so often expressed in print...The bar is
seen as a haven for social misfits.' (Jeffreys, p127). Indeed,
the lesbians at the House of Shades scarcely struggle

against their gloomy lot, display only muted anger and call their partners 'wife' or 'husband'. This aping of male attitudes, uneasy and mannered as it is, leads to some of the more ghastly and cringe-making moments in the novel – when, for example, Matt makes a joke about 'beating her wife' (p218), or Stag, an unrelenting butch, feels complimented by a girlfriend's remark that, 'The only difference between you and a man is that you wear deodorant' (p235). The best these women look forward to is 'a time when we can all be what individually we are and nobody gives a damn' (p236), but they do not seem to know how to achieve this aim. Some of the didactic passages turgidly declare what Jane Rule has called 'the weight of education which has imposed such a burden on Maureen Duffy's experience and style' (Rule, p182).

Nevertheless, an analysis does start to emerge from the contradictions. Matt herself has, for a deep thinker, a curiously unpolitical attitude to her search for the origins of her lesbian identity, but there are other characters who demonstrate an awareness of the restrictions imposed by a patriarchal society. '"I'm not against babies," says Sadie, "only the way you got to have them. What was it that little niece of Jon's said once, 'You could be a mummy and Jonnie [her woman lover] could be a daddy.'... Just goes to show kids aren't born with these ideas"' (p195). Over dinner with Stag and her lover, Irene, Matt relates the events leading up to the death of the ancient British queen Boadicea. When Matt finishes, Stag says, 'but what does it mean?' 'It was becoming a patriarchy with God the father that did for us,' replies Irene (pp234–5). Duffy's depiction of domestic violence is calculatedly shocking – 'clouting her round the earhole til she fell against the scullery wall and her face was the colour of dirty sheets not so much because of the pain, no... though he hurt her we could see that... but for the hurt inside' (p187).

I did not read *The Microcosm* myself until 1973, and I remember feeling both excited and depressed by it. My discovery of a nitty-gritty testament to what seemed to be 'real lesbian life' was thrilling, particularly because it seemed to embody a non-patriarchal narrative form. The aggressive linearity of conventional masculine prose often devalues women's experience, emphasises, in order to dismiss, its supposed inconsequentiality. By the time I read *The Microcosm*, I was already hooked on Virginia Woolf's cyclic fictions and Duffy seemed a natural heir to *her* style. While Duffy does not have a light touch with language, her layered, mannered prose seemed consistent with the thickly textured lives of her mainly working-class characters. But the novel depressed me too. I did not know if I could bear 'real lesbian life' to be *this* gritty, *this* drab, or for the unfolding cyclic patterns to reveal only the futility of existence.

Nevertheless, anger, that white-hot anger I and other lesbian feminists felt and acted with in the 1970s as we uncovered the extent of our oppression, is nascent in the novel, though so deeply embedded that it is heard only with very close attention. No doubt the inception of this novel, as a series of non-fiction case histories, allows the writer the get-out clause that she is simply reflecting what lesbians say about their lives. However, it *is* fiction and thus opens up the question of how lesbians *may* be represented. I believe that viewed within its historical period and despite that gloomy tone, *The Microcosm* is a valuable contribution to radical feminist explorations of lesbian existence. It is sometimes simplistic, often maddeningly miserable, but its decentralised narrative structure, which runs so seamlessly, even confusingly, from one character to another, creates a tension in the reader that she can only attempt to resolve by continual questioning of both text and self. In this respect this novel challenges us to recognise the contradictions and reversals experienced by lesbians in a male-dominated world. Importantly, *The Microcosm* paved the way for other lesbian writers, including Jeanette Winterson and Caeia March, to explore non-linear forms as more apt vehicles for their fictions.

My experience – of being both elated and depressed by *The Microcosm* – seems to be a common one for lesbian readers of lesbian fiction. Our expectations are very high, our needs great, and narrative fiction is often an important means to the construction of lesbian identity. How then does Caeia March's first novel, *Three Ply Yarn*, published in 1986, meet our needs and expectations? This novel played a key part in the beginning of a new wave of popular lesbian feminist fiction in Britain, and met a market anxious for depictions of lesbian lives. In my pub poll, several women had read *Three Ply Yarn* and her subsequent novel, *The Hide and Seek Files* (1988), more than once. They delighted in the accessible characters and said they read March's novels for sheer escapism into an agreeably consciousness-raised world. They appreciated, too, March's commitment to portraying the lives of working-class and black women, often notably absent from early feminist fiction.

March's literary intentions seem, in many respects, similar to Duffy's. Like *The Microcosm*, *Three Ply Yarn* addresses the lives of mainly working-class women (though not all of them are lesbians), and weaves these together through a particular narrative style. March has written of her desire 'for an economic form of language' and 'to use fiction to record the unrecorded examples' of women's lives (March, 1991, pp243–4). *Three Ply Yarn* uses diary entries, letters and transcribed tape recordings as devices to decentralise the narrative focus. The three main characters present their narratives out of chronological sequence – from Esther's 1980s diary to Deanne's memories of the 1950s to Lotte's present-day experiences – which breaks up the traditional linear plot-line. There are problems with this technique. At times all three voices, or narratives, have a similar pace and rhythm, and sometimes the characterisation can seem two-dimensional. When March remarks in her explication of 'The Process of Writing *Three Ply Yarn*' that she 'was writing a novel not an essay', she identifies one of the difficulties for all writers of overtly political fiction (March, 1991, p246). Narratives and characters need to be very skilfully constructed if ideological messages are to be digested comfortably by the reader.

March has made her ideological position in *Three Ply Yarn* very clear. She 'wanted the novel to challenge patriarchy, both patriarchy as a system, and patriarchy as represented by individuals...any man can be a representative of patriarchy' (March, 1991, p244). So while March's novel is sometimes as didactic as *The Microcosm*, there has been a more concerted attempt to clarify the political issues. When Dora, Deanne's first lover, is institutionalised in a mental hospital, March combines both the general polemic on the hidden oppression of women by the system, and the specific personal experience: 'The official cause of death was heart failure. I know she died of terror when men came at her with their cables and electrodes' (March, 1986, p53). Lotte's experience of domestic violence is conveyed through the frightened empathetic imaginings of Deanne: 'I was getting distress signals coming through like waves...I was four floors away from their room' (p134). The reticence of Lotte's mother-in-law in confronting her son's violence rings true: ' "I'm sorry, Lotte, that my son could have done this." Lotte just turned her head away. Sandra Slomner might be sorry but she would never let this spoil James Junior's chances in the firm' (p136).

March's approach works best when the politics are integrated into the plot. It is not always so successful when a character articulates an opinion. In an argument between Esther and her new lover, Chris, Esther launches into a diatribe against Freud: 'Freud, for example...didn't believe that men could actually abuse their power. So he made their actions into women's fantasies. You can't get more male than that. It's a typical male ploy' (p180). While this passage would be reasonable in a political article, it seems too heavy with polemics for a novel or a lovers' argument. My pub readers agreed that, even in radical feminist households, these kind of disputes usually revolve around the *really* important issues like who should empty the cat litter, who ate the last chocolate bourbon and so on. March perhaps mistakenly presupposes a lack of awareness on the part of her readership. However, she began writing during a time of political debate when there was considered, among lesbian feminists, to be a need to proselytise, and the awkwardness of these passages may reflect the conflict between traditional narrative forms and emerging political beliefs.

Three Ply Yarn illustrates the dilemma confronting the writer of political novels. How far should she reflect the current status quo, the language and self-presentation of her contemporaries, and how far should she introduce new realities, attempt to transcend the boundaries of patriarchal existence? Does she owe any duty to her readers and if so what kind of duty? March clearly sees a political duty 'to challenge patriarchy', but fiction is fickle. It does not like being contained by ideological boundaries and even the most hide-bound of patriarchs cannot control his reader's observations. March acknowledges her predicament in her account of the production of *Three Ply Yarn*. She writes of a feeling that the plot and characters of the novel had been dictated to her by an external force: 'As the women in *Three Ply Yarn* unfolded on to paper, they fascinated me . . . I was amazed at how the women argued with me, refusing to co operate if I interfered too much. Often they took me completely by surprise' (March, 1991, p251). March is in good company with this observation. Charlotte Brontë apparently experienced similar mystical interventions more than 150 years ago, when 'phantasms . . . conjured from nothing, – from nothing to a system strange as some religious creed' came rushing upon her (Peters, p50).

This phenomenon may be used to absolve the writer of responsibility for her creations. If her characters give the wrong impression, sometimes speak out of turn or use a jarring or unpopular tone, it is not the writer's fault. Both Brontë and March seem to have experienced a crisis of confidence when writing in their own authority, despite in other respects being authoritative figures. Such crises may arise from transgressing accepted boundaries, as the nineteenth-century poet Robert Southey clearly indicated in his advice to Brontë: 'Literature cannot be the business of a woman's life, and it ought not to be' (Peters, p54).

Duffy's novels, significantly, demonstrate a confident authorial voice. We might perhaps locate this confidence in Duffy's apparent identification with a patriarchal literary hierarchy. At a 1996 conference on autobiography at Warwick University I heard Duffy firmly declare that 'The Author is *not* dead!' (12 October 1996). The Author so often implies a man whose position in the world makes him right all the time – Tolstoy, Freud, Southey, Tolkien – that it might be better for women if He *were* dead. But Duffy is not so attached to a male literary tradition that she is afraid to subvert its subjects. Her novels are often savagely critical of patriarchal society. *Love Child* (1971), for example, gives an acerbic portrait of a father who is distant, controlled and controlling, expects unobtrusive service from his wife, loyalty from his employees and good entertainment value from his child. The father is, importantly, the only figure in the novel to be unequivocally himself, gendered, classed. His power to control the lives and identities of those around him is never in doubt. One of his adolescent offspring's ironic nicknames for him is 'Allthing'. This precocious, watchful teenager, Kit, is the first-person narrator throughout the novel (which this time has a plot-led form). Duffy never reveals Kit's gender or sexual identity, nor that of Ajax, secretary to Kit's father, lover of Kit's mother. Without the usual gendered signposts the reader has to struggle to construct the meaning of the novel. Is Kit a girl who is jealous of her mother's male lover? Or is Kit's mother having an affair with a woman? Maybe Kit is a boy? *Love Child* has reverberated through many subsequent fictions. In Winterson's most recent novel, *Gut Symmetries* (1997), the lonely adolescent vigilance of Alice looks like a tribute to Kit, even to her epiphany in a catch of sardine. Whichever gender we allot to Kit, the damage patriarchal power relations cause to both women and men, girls and boys, is evident.

Caeia March also looks at the performance of gender in her second novel, *The Hide and Seek Files*, published in

1988. Biff is a lesbian who, because of persecution as a suffragette, takes on the clothing and persona of a man. Her lifelong passing in that role, as the seemingly heterosexual partner of Moss, as local businessman, step-grandfather and a bloke among other blokes, is successful. After the immediate threat of imprisonment diminishes, Biff continues to maintain her disguise. Her sex remains undiscovered even after death owing to Moss' vigilance. Where Matt's butchness in *The Microcosm* is problematised for lesbian feminist readers now, March rests her analysis of Biff's cross-dressing on the particular historical circumstances. Yet Matt and Biff are similar. Both adopt roles as a survival technique founded on their experience of what is available. True, Biff offers nothing but pragmatic reasons for her role-playing, and Matt tends to philosophise hers. But in daily life Matt experiences the hostility of a homophobic world, while Biff, as long as her disguise holds, is accorded the status and respect owing to a man. March is non-directive and leaves us to draw our own ideological conclusions about Biff's passing identity, which, despite our being in on the secret, has a strange and convincing ambivalence in the novel.

March's portrayal of Biff is subtle and sympathetic. Her representation of Frank, a 'good, kind, honest man and hardworking', who lived alone with his mother before marrying Moss, is less successful. March describes him as 'boring...without any sense of his own worth', and a 'shadow of what he could have been if he had only left Herton, his parents, the shop, and gone out to see the world' (p32). Frank's lack of a strong masculine identity is characterised as a negative aspect of his personality. The problem here is that a rough division of men into machismo swine or weak but fairly decent blokes neither reveals the problematic potential for misogyny in decent blokes nor the complexity and variety of male violence. We end up then with a kind of cultural stereotyping that mocks the unmanly shopkeeper and, in the pit strikes at the end of *The Hide and Seek Files*, tends to glorify the coal miner. The strength of this novel lies, not in its characterisation, but in its powerful narrative that speaks the silences in lesbian history. Adrienne Rich has written that 'Women's love for women has been represented almost entirely through silence and lies' and that 'Heterosexuality...has also drowned in silence the erotic feelings between women' (Rich, p190). When Biff hears Frank propose marriage over the dinner table to the pregnant Moss, she cannot speak: 'The silence could have cut the meat in paper-thin slices' (p35). But March examines modes of recovery of both silences and 'erotic feelings' between women: 'Love of Moss consumed Biff. Lying awake at night, thinking of Moss, knowing what love there could be, if only. If only' (p35).

Duffy, like March, is resolutely anti-patriarchy and she offers analyses of male power that accord with radical feminist readings. The imagery and narrative in a more recent novel, *Illuminations* (1991), startlingly suggest a global conspiracy of misogyny, although in this novel the patriarchy seems scarcely dented by the preceding years of feminist activity. Two key images dominate the novel: the violent and meaningless killing of a fox and a cat, and the myth of the rape of Europa. The atmosphere of fear in which Duffy's two principal female characters live is chillingly believable. We recognise how exhausting is the ordinary business of our daily lives, work, shopping, visiting friends, in a misogynist world. These middle-class academics have good incomes and expenses-paid trips to conferences, but their money and status hold good only as long as they are good. Helge, the German lesbian who gets involved in social revolutionary politics, is pursued by sinister men from an anti-terrorist agency and betrayed by her male comrades. Hetty, a rather staid English academic, is passed over as head of department at her college in favour of a man. In a sort of mid-life crisis she stops having affairs with men and subsequently falls in love with Helge at a conference in Brussels where 'most of the delegates are men in suits...with here and there a conspicuous woman' (pp48–9). We follow Hetty's politicisation as she becomes the subject of police interest herself, her phone tapped, her letters opened. There is a symbolic moment when Hetty goes to her local pub alone and is immediately approached by 'a man in a donkey jacket' who demands her attention. Hetty feels obliged to 'smile, as if in agreement' with his monologue, 'though questioning silently whether that, after all, is the secret of the "Mona Lisa" and if her enigmatic gaze is just the posture women have been taught, by example, to assume while men assail them' (p38). The donkey-jacket man becomes an emblem of an enduring and violent misogyny that extends from the torturing to death of a cat to the rape of a young girl. The police suspiciously scrutinise Hetty's research into the letters of an eighth-century German nun in case they contain coded revolutionary messages. Ironically, the police are incapable of perceiving the letters' true subversive content.

As the novel progresses, Hetty, with her new insight into the workings of male power, sees the destruction of the female everywhere. When she looks at the moon she sees 'Diana raped by a rocket and rubberised men gambolling weightless in their heavy boots' and wonders 'what can we fill the universe with...now that the goddesses have packed up and gone away' (p96). Watching television she is 'beaten down by images of violence and despair' (p141). When she listens to the carol 'The Holly and the Ivy', it occurs to her that 'once there must have been more verses about the ivy, male and female alternating' (p217).

Ideologically this is a gloomier message even than that of *The Microcosm*. The women in *Illuminations* are isolated, alone or diffidently coupling. There is no sense of women organising resistance against the destruction of themselves and the planet. Rather than fight – and the odds do seem overwhelmingly against them – the women go underground. Helge is sacked, Hetty gives up her job, and they buy a little place in France. Hetty is politicised, yes, but only when it is too late. Like Europa, she did not start fighting soon enough, and she has been compromised by her complicity in the system. At the end of the novel,

Hetty sits in the National Gallery in front of Veronese's painting *The Rape of Europa*, 'attempting to resolve its ambiguities. Are the waiting women trying to dissuade Europa or helping her on to the bull's back?' This spine-tingling observation begs the central question in *Illuminations*. What are we doing in the face of the threat to our existence? Sadly, for the women in this novel there are only personal survival solutions.

The word 'survivor' crops up again in Caeia March's latest novel, *Between the Worlds* (1996), which, significantly in the light of Rich's metaphor of the drowning of lesbian eroticism by heterosexuality, begins with a lesbian contemplating suicide by casting herself into the sea. Lerryn, last heard of in *The Hide and Seek Files*, is found drunk, staring out over a Cornish bay. She has filled bags with stones to weight herself down in the water and only her excessive intake of brandy, and the appearance on the clifftop of two lesbians from the local women's land, Cherry and Beech, save her from carrying out her intention. Lerryn therefore becomes a survivor. Similarly, Tarn, Lerryn's eventual lover, frequently describes herself and her daughter as survivors.

The lesbian community in *Between the Worlds* is also a survivor, despite threats from selfish children and a changing economy. March uses myths and fairy tales to give a sense of historical and spiritual continuity to the lives of her characters. The device lends an airy, fragmentary quality to the novel and is educative without being sternly didactic, but it can have its pitfalls. Mythology and folklore do not always subvert the patriarchal status quo. For example, in March's own account of Rhiannon, who was kidnapped by the King of Dyfed, she employs the euphemistic words, 'he had tricked her into marrying him' and 'eventually, she became pregnant', romanticising what seems to be a symbolic story of capture and rape (p195). There is, however, an engaging cheerfulness about the frequent fairy-tale episodes that is absent from the present-day narrative.

When things get tough at the political coal-face, it is always possible, as Duffy has shown in *Illuminations*, to shift the narrative via a fictive research project to an earlier historical period heavy with ideological parallels to the present. A number of recent novels, like A. S. Byatt's *Possession: A Romance* (1990) and Carol Shields' *Mary Swann* (1987), have employed this device. In *Between the Worlds*, it is Tarn's friend Liesl who provides the antique German connection. Liesl is researching the fourteenth-century Beguines women's religious community in Cologne and uncovers some ancient tiles inscribed by an order member. This technique, in both *Between the Worlds* and *Illuminations*, emphasises that, in olden times, sometimes things were just as bad as now and sometimes they were better. Either way, it provides a distraction from dealing with the present.

The present in *Between the Worlds* yields only a limited optimism, though it does not have quite the doom-laden air of *Illuminations*. The tenants of the Cornish women's land are served an eviction notice when one of its two women owners decides to sell up. The land had been tacitly understood 'to be held in perpetuity for women' and the tenants understandably feel betrayed, but at the end of the novel a new women's land is found (p68). Like *Three Ply Yarn*, the narrative threads of *Between the Worlds* are divided between a number of characters, and like *The Microcosm* its narrative may be suddenly disrupted by the recounting of a fairy tale or piece of local folklore. The slow pace and episodic fragmentary quality of March's earlier novels tended to produce a positive forward-moving effect, but *Between the Worlds* has, in common with *Illuminations*, a sense of women's world-weariness and retreat from active confrontation with the patriarchal world into personal spiritual resolutions.

So, have the writings of Duffy and March changed since their first novels were published? I believe they have. *Illuminations* and *Between the Worlds* show that both writers have shifted their ideological positions. Duffy seems more focused, analytical, her criticisms of patriarchal forms more overt, and yet, as I have suggested, the political resolution she offers is one of individual survival. Interestingly, *Illuminations* appears to forgo literary experiment, and its structure, though episodic, is similar to any number of other contemporary novels. Perhaps this is because, as Duffy hoped, the novel itself is now less grounded in linear narrative and central plot. Maybe the novel has caught up with Duffy. Although March has retained both the decentred form that characterises *Three Ply Yarn* and a sense of women's solidarity and community, the urgency of her storylines, perhaps influenced by the current social and political climate, seems to have been lost. She has not abandoned her earlier feminist vision of a world, but the realisation of this vision is less imminent and more restricted in *Between the Worlds*. In this novel too, the emphasis is on survival. The raw vitality of narrative, characterisation and style in the earlier works of both novelists allow for greater possibilities of change and renewal. The women in *Illuminations* and *Between the Worlds* may be more observant of power relations, better equipped to analyse them, but they have all, it seems, entered into an era in which feminist energy is concentrated on personal survival, where 'everything happens in an eternal present', as Duffy wrote of her microcosmic tribe of lesbians. While we are all survivors in some respects, the later writings of Duffy and March give us a timely reminder that, in an ideological struggle, the role of survivor may ultimately be as restricting as that of victim, and that we need plural forms of the verb to be if we are to grasp the concept of lesbian existence, past, present and future.

REFERENCES

Novels

Byatt, A. S., *Possession: A Romance*, Vintage, London, 1990

Duffy, Maureen (1966), *The Microcosm*, Virago, London, 1989 edn

—(1971), *Love Child*, Virago, London, 1994 edn

—(1991), *Illuminations*, Flamingo, London, 1992 edn

March, Caeia, *Three Ply Yarn*, The Women's Press, London, 1986

—, *The Hide and Seek Files*, The Women's Press, London, 1988

—, *Between the Worlds*, The Women's Press, London, 1996

Shields, Carol (1987), *Mary Swann*, Flamingo, London, 1990

Winterson, Jeanette, *Art & Lies*, Vintage, London, 1995

—, *Gut Symmetries*, Granta, London, 1997

Other References

Jeffreys, Sheila, *The Lesbian Heresy: A Feminist Perspective on the Lesbian Revolution*, The Women's Press, London, 1994

March, Caeia, 'The Process of Writing *Three Ply Yarn*', in Elaine Hobby and Chris White, eds, *What Lesbians Do in Books*, The Women's Press, London, 1991

Peters, Margot, *Unquiet Soul: A Biography of Charlotte Brontë*, Hodder and Stoughton, London, 1987

Rich, Adrienne, 'Women and Honour: Some Notes on Lying', in *On Lies, Secrets and Silence: Selected Prose 1966–1978*, Virago, London, 1980

Rule, Jane, *Lesbian Images*, Peter Davies, London, 1976

WOEBEGONE DYKES: THE NOVELS OF LISA ALTHER

Vada Hart

Walk through any high-street bookshop and you will see books piled high, selling cheap. Fierce competition in the book trade has led to price wars and cost-cutting. Books have become a commodity and what matters is rapid turnover and profit margins. Combined with the retreat of feminism, not to mention feminist writers, to the academy, this intense commercial pressure has made it harder and harder for the surviving feminist publishers to swim against the mainstream tide. Indeed, during the 1990s, the women's presses have, to some extent, dabbled in the mainstream, publishing more and more genre fiction, such as lesbian whodunnits and romances, less and less that is explicitly radical. Financial pressure to compromise has always been there, but is now stronger than ever, while it is becoming increasingly difficult to express and sustain feminist politics. There is a strong demand for bestsellers, fast-sellers, and, by definition, these will be in tune with majority taste. At best, authors may seek to educate and refine that taste, to push out boundaries, at worst they may collude with hetero-patriarchal values, heterosexism, male violence, anti-lesbianism and anti-feminism.

Bestsellers may sometimes include lesbian themes and characters, but they are unlikely to reflect radical feminist values, unless in a distorting mirror, and they are equally unlikely to foreground lesbians in a positive light. Susanne Kappeler has argued that the suppression of feminist ideas in Western capitalist patriarchies is achieved through control of the market rather than through legislation. How this works in practice is that mainstream publishers publish and promote authors who write about lesbians only if they do not portray lesbian existence as a threatening alternative to compulsory heterosexuality. Similarly, novels may have a prominent lesbian theme, but only so long as the context is gloom and doom, with the characters eventually consigned to well-deserved oblivion.

I propose to examine this phenomenon by looking closely at the work of one well-known writer, though my argument could equally be applied to others. Lisa Alther has written bestsellers, mainly published by mainstream publishers, throughout the last two decades, virtually reflecting the lifespan of the women's movement. Lesbian themes recur in all her books and are central to some of them. Nevertheless, many women readers express surprise when this is pointed out to them, as if they had not registered her writing as, in some important sense, lesbian. Why this may be, we shall see.

Alther's literary achievement is not in question. Her work is complex, funny, entertaining and often topical. Her style is elegant. Her novels are carefully plotted sagas of women's lives from cradle to middle age, their relationships, the setbacks they encounter, their changes of direction. It is easy to see their appeal, as women's perceptions are central. To read as a lesbian, however, is to have a particular perspective, to be aware of negative representations of lesbians and concerned at their harmful effects. How, then, does Alther portray her lesbian characters? And how does she treat lesbian and feminist themes?

Alther's novels have a female voice and are mainly concerned with the identity and experiences of particular, middle-class American women. But despite the subject matter, her work is not threatening to male and mainstream publishers. It is interesting that an American academic and lesbian, Margaret Kissam Morris, in a review of *Five Minutes in Heaven* (1995) which includes an excellent overview of the earlier novels, refers at length to their entertainment value as works of popular fiction, with 'plots that sustain middle-class values without examining the nature of those values' (Morris, p23).

Kinflicks (1976), Alther's first novel, was a popular fiction bestseller. A formidable saga, the novel follows the fortunes of Ginny Babcock, from her early days in Tennessee to the point where, after a botched suicide attempt, doomed to survival, she packs her knapsack and heads out into the unknown. Though Ginny has heterosexual relationships and marries, there are strongly lesbian-related themes. At college, Ginny becomes the protégée of Miss Head, the spinster stereotype in person, whose cerebral interests do not extend far beyond Descartes and playing the cello. Their relationship remains strictly platonic. Poor benighted Miss Head serves the literary purpose of enabling Ginny to move on from her redneck boyfriend to a racy affair with Edna (Eddie) Holzer, a statuesque left-wing activist given to strumming her guitar and singing 'Mr Tambourine Man' when not whittling away at her sensuous sculptures. In no time they are in bed. Ginny rushes off at once to tell Miss Head, intent on saving her from living death by academia, announcing, 'I'm a lesbian. I spent all last night making love to Eddie Holzer...And it was wonderful' (p268). Ginny and Eddie move in together. 'I had to keep reminding myself that I was now officially a "lesbian"' (p302). Ginny notices public disapproval when she holds hands in the street with her lover, so, immediately, the perspective of the heterosexual world is introduced. Together the women go to every demonstration they hear of. Lest we should take the relationship and the activism too seriously, a turning point is introduced. The women's apartment is condemned, so they move to rural Vermont. Here they live among a community of heavily satirised hippies, while their neighbours are the redneck denizens of Stark's Bog, a small town. The women try to bring feminism to Stark's Bog, opening a family-planning centre and holding a women's weekend. There is a throwaway reference to Eddie's radical analysis of male power: 'Eddie took further comfort in the fact that we were boycotting one aspect of the corrupt male power structure that was perpetrating all the misery in the world by seeking our sexual fulfilment elsewhere' (p314), which immediately trivialises her politics. This book was, after all, written during the earlier days of the women's movement, when sexual fulfilment was seen as important, as was, indeed, separating from men sexually and emotionally.

References to the peace campaign, civil rights, draft-dodging and the Vietnam War set the scene of the era. Ginny is embarrassed that her money comes from the family arms factory, but no political issue is allowed to assume too much importance, or to escape the scatter-gun satire. The uppity dyke becomes inconvenient to the plot, so poor Eddie literally loses her head in a gory accident. Then, with indecent haste, Ginny goes off with Ira, the fire officer and snowmobile salesman, because she feels a need for order in her life. A month after seeing her lover decapitated, she gets married. In this novel, then, the lesbians come to a sad end, left behind, written out, killed off. The book did have a readership among lesbian feminists, but it does not seem to have had the impact of some other, contemporary novels, like *The Women's Room* (1977) or *Woman on the Edge of Time* (1976). Unlike these books, which took their politics seriously, it would hardly have changed lives, or indeed minds. The humour is worn almost as a mask. The tone seems deeply ambivalent. Ultimately it suggests small-town life and values may not be so bad; radicals, intellectuals and lesbian feminists are ridiculous.

The civil rights movement, women's liberation and trade unionism also play some part in *Original Sins* (1981), which follows the lives of five children from Tennessee. Here too the tone is unfailingly satirical, in case any reader might be tempted to take all that radicalism seriously. The novel's lesbian character, Emily, grows up studious and lacking in pep, unlike her cheerleader sister, Sally, who marries early and becomes a small-town housewife. For Emily the die may be cast when, as a girl, she thrills at the passing touch of the repressed games mistress. But she works her way through various male idealists and activists and eventually marries. The novel reflects the atmosphere of the early women's movement; Emily has become involved in a consciousness-raising group. She falls in love with Maria in that context and eventually dismisses her husband. Maria is well observed as a civil rights worker; disillusioned with men, she thinks it would be difficult to go back to them. Here, as elsewhere in her novels, Alther shows a sharp awareness of the feminist debates concerning heterosexuality, male power and male violence, but while radical feminist politics feature as a strand in the narrative, the entire structure of the novel, moving as it does between several characters, prevents it being centre stage and also allows the author to stand aside.

Emily is depicted as having difficulties with her lover's non-monogamous lifestyle, but is influenced by her analysis of male power: 'She kept trying to make exceptions for "her" man. But Maria was right. There could be no exceptions. They all profited from each act performed by other men that kept women afraid and at their service' (p460). By the end of the novel, Emily has come out to her sister at the latter's husband's funeral. Emily feels that Sally is pleased that she has finally been upfront, but in another chapter we discover that she is mistaken and her sister's real reaction was disgust at being told things she did not want to hear at an inappropriate time. Immediately we have the small-town view of Emily, as self-centred and deluded. The perspective has shifted, not only on the character but also, to an extent, on the radical feminist politics she has adopted, which is perhaps an indication of the author's own ambivalence.

At the funeral Emily suffers 'her own grief at the brevity and difficulty of life' (p460) and longs for Maria to hold her, 'touch her and gently stroke life back into her numb body' (p461). She looks forward to the help and sympathy she

will get from her women's group. They will support her
desire to live and struggle on behalf of the downtrodden
women of the world, so that none of their daughters would
have to go through what Emily's sister was enduring.
Alther cuts through the narrative of idealistic hopes with
a paragraph describing the gospel quartet at the funeral
singing about the one-way flight to the glory land. The
novel closes with a second generation of children,
offspring of the original protagonists, playing together as
their parents had done, in an old 'witchlike' tree. Their
parents look on. The black father says, 'Gon to be different
for them.' 'Damn right,' snarled Emily. 'Lots of luck,'
muttered Raymond, the political activist (pp590–91).
Raymond might be voicing Alther's own disillusionment
and cynicism here: change is less than likely.

This dismissal of hopes for the liberation of women as
unrealistic, pie-in-the-sky hot-gospel promises, just about
sums up the tenor of the novel. It's witty, satirical, but
often at the expense of women, like working-class Sally
with her ridiculous crafts projects and the almost
stereotypical abused, downtrodden black women. It ends
where it started, with a backward look. The tension
throughout Original Sins, between radical and feminist
hopes and aspirations and small-town conservatism and
fatalism, is not fully or optimistically resolved. The
activists, including the lesbian characters, remain on the
margins. They are not about to transform society.

Whereas Original Sins is a long saga of life in the 1950s
and 1960s, Other Women deals with one woman and her
conflicts. Published in 1984, it reflects what was going on
in the United States at that time, when therapy was very
much in the ascendant, deradicalising and depoliticising
lesbians, as more and more women sought to change their
heads rather than change the world. The novel seems to be
straightforwardly pro-therapy, at that time still very much
a sacred cow, and for once the satire is muted. This novel
reflects the beginnings of the backlash, which became the
new queer politics and theory. Rather than making
political choices, some lesbians began to see themselves as

a 'gay' sexual minority, with a number even defining themselves as perverts, as does Caroline, the main character in *Other Women*. A middle-aged nurse and lesbian mother, she is in the midst of an identity crisis, having tried all kinds of solutions, including marriage and feminism. Therapy remains untried, so she embarks on a long course of sessions with the tedious Hannah, who appears to be meant to be a sympathetic character. Hannah passes her spare moments reading pulp romances, because they have happy endings and turn her on. She seems to have amazing insight and is constantly offering interpretations of what is in her client's mind. Caroline might be unsure of her own thoughts, but that poses no problem for Hannah. Liberal and a touch Freudian, she announces that we are all bisexual; we make choices based on social pressures and family dynamics. Caroline insists that being a lesbian did not feel like a choice, even though she has already had heterosexual relationships. Hannah diagnoses her problem as always taking a caring role, hence the difficulties with her lover, Diana. They are just too nice to each other. Caroline slogs on with the therapy, even as her relationship crumbles and her lover has an affair with a younger woman.

Caroline is represented as totally confused; uncertain whether to opt for Brian, heterosexual privilege and bourgeois American life, with a new baby and pina coladas by the swimming pool...or to continue as a lesbian. Her feminist experience does not seem to help her insights or her decisions. In the past, she worked on an abortion-referral project, but left, descending into despair over the problems involved. She has two friends from that era, Pam and Jenny, who do as little work as possible, and have as many simultaneous lovers as possible, feeling that this undermines patriarchy and builds up matriarchy. Caroline is too inhibited by her Boston puritan heritage to follow suit, but she does go to a health club Pam told her about, where she picks up a woman and has a brief sexual encounter, at last untrammelled by her destructive pattern of caring too much. Here, the characters appear to be imitating gay male sexual practice, which illustrates how Alther is very quick to reflect trends.

Though Pam and Jenny appear to be travesties of feminists, the novel does make serious feminist points on the issue of male violence. Caroline is very aware of this problem, since she spends her life patching up the women and children who have suffered its effects. She berates her therapist for sheltering under the benefits of white male privilege. Hannah takes this as evidence of a step forward in therapy, an expression of independence, but she does acknowledge some of the criticism. She comes to see that her pulp romances brainwash women to view their rapists and murderers as protectors, and she burns them. She also starts to wonder what life would be like with another woman, though she remains cosily married. Her client, of course, develops a transference relationship with Hannah, though she knows her task is to move on and let go.

By the end of the novel Caroline is represented as being 'in recovery', and she has become Hannah's friend (no more than that) instead of her patient. She has also made a final break with Diana, her lover. The central lesbian relationship appears to be displaced by the interaction with the therapist. Paradoxically, the lesbian relationship is depicted as neurotic, though it is described by Alther in a manner which suggests much warmth, love and equality. One wonders why Caroline and Diana would not have been able to work something out, and why the therapist would not have seen some value in their relationship. I find it disconcerting that Hannah constantly dismisses Caroline's social concerns and caring as neurotic symptoms and destructive patterns. *Other Women* ends with a promise of summer, and Hannah wondering, as well she might, what Caroline will become.

Bedrock (1990) is also concerned with the relationship between two women, Clea, a photographer, and Elke, a deeply gloomy sculptress. This novel attracted some bad reviews in England, along the lines of 'yet another wacky book about lesbians and alternative lifestyles...' but it remains well within the realm of the mainstream. Alther's underlying ideology seems to have moved in the direction of sexual libertarianism. The novel's heavier satirical passages depict a separatist, matriarchal commune. Both Clea and Elke are married to accommodating men. Clea is physically and emotionally drawn to Elke. Once, they attempted a sexual expression of their attraction, but this was not a success. The desire subsided, but a passionate attachment remained. The narrative develops from Clea's move away from her husband to Roches Ridge, Vermont (a small country town populated by ill-assorted rednecks, eccentrics, lesbians and gay men, very similar to Stark's Bog in *Kinflicks*), into a saga of life, death and graveyard humour. A group of lesbians, the Boudiccas, live in tepees in the creek below Clea's house. They don't like men. They are rumoured to have killed their rooster. Alther's depiction of this group leaves little doubt about her view of lesbian separatists. The Boudiccas have names like Starshine, Foxglove and Morning Glory and are given to dancing naked around camp fires, beating drums and striking karate stances. Starshine has a parrot which shrieks embarrassingly passé slogans such as 'Make love, not war!', 'We shall overcome!' and 'Che Guevara', but the poor bird cannot learn to say, 'The personal is political.' Funny, yes, but also a device by means of which radical and feminist politics are collapsed into the wilder excesses of matriarchal and separatist groups, and thereby reduced to the level of mere parroted slogans.

The Roches Ridge lesbian and gay communities are presented as ridiculous, narcissistic and part and parcel of the oddness of a very peculiar town. There is what appears to be a more positive moment when Clea's daughter comes out as a lesbian, but after a summer at Greenham Common the offspring turns up with a suitable Yale boyfriend in chinos and penny loafers. (Just a passing phase). But the love which never quite speaks its name lingers on between Clea and Elke, who put a good deal of energy into holding off from each other, for fear their husbands will suffer, as might Clea's children. Elke, ill with desire for Clea, sublimates it into her agonised sculptures, which seem to owe something to Käthe Kollwitz. Terence, her husband, sees her as increasingly determined to flee the coop. At length, realising that she and Clea are becoming grey-haired and menopausal, Elke propositions Clea, offering a one-off experience before they die. Together they enjoy a dramatic interlude, complete with hot flushes in the sunset, after their twenty years of building up to this moment. They do not repeat the experience, despite their passion, since, as Alther writes, they both had other things to do.

The Boudiccas, meanwhile, hire a therapist to help them sort out why they tend to get taken over by matriarchal authority figures. In a well-worn parody of feminist process, they come to a consensus to reach all future decisions by consensus. Clea eventually bows out, having found a new ability to sit quiet and be alone. Can this be the dawning of new age? *Bedrock* is, on the whole, a darkly funny book, with hints of Evelyn Waugh and perhaps Anna Livia, but for this lesbian reader it is all too much a dead end, like Roches Ridge itself, a long narrative of frustration and closet romance, culminating in nothing much.

'Looking for love in all the wrong places' announces the cheery cover of the paperback edition of *Five Minutes in Heaven* (1995). This is the story of Jude, who grew up in Tennessee in the 1950s, and the main theme is her 'graveyard love', enduring beyond death, of various unsuitable and frustrating individuals. Though set mainly in the past, the novel reflects the current ambience of queer politics and vogue for postmodernism.

In *Five Minutes*, lesbians stay in the closet. Jude learns to pass early on, when she is teased because of her close relationship with her best friend, Molly. Though the pair have a brief moment of physicality, sharing a bed as adolescents, this is later denied by Molly, who rejects such behaviour as wrong. Molly is fatally injured in a car crash and becomes the first of Jude's graveyard loves. Memories of Molly intrude into Jude's adult relationships, warning her off. Jude gradually moves towards a consciousness of her lesbianism through her attachments to two gay men,

Sandy, her childhood companion, and Simon, his lover. Interestingly, when everyone else is out celebrating in the streets after Stonewall, Jude and Sandy are indoors, sleeping together. At the beginning of the gay liberation movement, their agenda does not involve politics. Neither character is exclusively heterosexual or gay, but they are being co-opted into heterosexual activity – yet another example of authorial ambivalence, despite Alther's apparent sympathy with gay lifestyles.

Sandy soon reaps the fruit of his thrill-seeking quest for anonymous gay sex. Beaten up in a homophobic attack, he dies and becomes another graveyard love. Later Jude meets Anna, a married woman writer. Despite a warning that Anna was bad news, and her own initial doubts, she comes to feel that with this lover she can re-create the happiness she had once known with Molly, in a return to the paradise of childhood. Sadly, Anna always goes back to Jim, her husband. Jude gradually realises that Anna has a drink problem, and when drunk can become a snarling beast. Moreover, she has a masochistic relationship with Jim, who beats her up. Jude fails to rescue Anna from Jim's clutches. Her reluctant perception is that Anna is colluding with him, since he supports her financially and she is a lazy woman. Alther makes it clear that there were very good times in the relationship between Jude and Anna, but the depiction of break-up and decline is depressing. Soon Anna too bites the dust, dying somewhat in the tortured manner of Zola's *Nana*, covered in sores, presumably the result of her drinking (or is there a hint of metaphor for some nameless and sinister disease?).

After Anna's death, Jude goes to France to work in publishing. Surrounded by postmodernist discoursing French women who play mind-games, Jude finds her Southern propensity for graveyard love begin to run amok. She goes to a strip club with her boss and male escorts, then later sees one of the performers, Olivia (spot the reference?). Olivia leads her on for a brief moment, then disappears. In a fit of mad passion, Jude pursues Olivia until the performer relents and sleeps with her, just once, though it is made clear that it is a meaningless act for this woman. After considering jumping in the Seine, Jude retreats underground to the Catacombs, an old burial place, intending to take an overdose. Instead, she falls asleep and struggles out after two days. The resurgent Jude goes back to the USA, cheered to think that although those she had loved were largely illusions of her own making, the love she felt for them was real and would even survive her (p371). As the novel closes, she is flirting with a stewardess, whose lipstick is described as co-ordinating with her gold and scarlet scarf. Naturally, she has deep blue eyes. After the graveyard loves, we seem to have moved to the realm of lipstick lesbian romance.

Here and there in the book there are references to feminist politics, but when Jude goes to a feminist book fair in London she finds the event has less to do with books than with feminism, and notes all the splits, the women of colour being angry with the white women, working-class women with middle-class women, lesbians with heterosexuals and everyone with men. Jude stands outside this and does not seem to see herself as a feminist. It may be that there is a subtext here and in the other novels concerning pre-feminist lesbians continuing as a sexual minority, distinct from argumentative, man-hating, collectivised radical feminists and lesbian separatists. These non-political women aspire to passionate but sometimes casual and uncommitted sex, glamour and, no doubt, co-ordinating lipstick. It is not clear what will become of Jude. The ending of the novel is fairly upbeat, but for lesbian readers the overall impression it makes is perhaps less than positive.

Alther's lesbian characters are seldom out of the closet and they regularly return to and have relationships with men. They settle for one-off (lesbian) stands, episodes between long separations. There is a definite tendency for them to get hurt and even die, once the nature of their sexuality is apparent. This is traditional stuff, but disappointing to the lesbian feminist reader. At a time when there is all too much death-oriented gay male fiction, the message seems to be that lesbians too may suffer for their sexuality, even end horribly, as Anna does in the last novel. Alther shows an awareness of the splits around sexuality, but appears to be on the side of queer politics, sexual libertarianism and gay male agendas. On the positive side, there is some critique of male violence in all the novels, from the horrors perpetrated by the gang of rednecks in *Kinflicks* to the abusive husbands in *Original Sins*, *Other Women* and *Five Minutes in Heaven*. (And yet... it has to be said that Alther frequently uses violent episodes to move the plot along.)

Lisa Alther returns again and again to lesbian themes, keeping lesbians, to some extent, in the mainstream, but the message I hear is very mixed. She is ambivalent about her lesbian characters and side-steps issues of sexual politics. Several of her characters seek solace in personal, inward solutions such as therapy or meditation. While Alther may be gently mocking their choices, the satire is too blunted to be radical, the humour too near to flippancy. There seems to be a wariness of offending the general reader, a response, I think, to market pressures. The effect of this position, however, is to reinforce harmful ideologies about lesbians and feminism, and we have to ask whose interests this stance serves.

It is to be hoped that Alther's next novel will present some positive lesbian images. So far she has set her books in the fairly recent past, contextualising them with references to current issues. Whether she will go on to deal more optimistically with feminists surviving academia, the backlash, new age, postmodernism and the new world order remains to be seen, but it is to be hoped that at least some of the dykes will be written as wonderful rather than weird and woebegone.

REFERENCES

Novels

Alther, Lisa (1976), *Kinflicks*, Penguin Books, Harmondsworth, 1977 edn

—, *Original Sins*, The Women's Press, London, 1981

— (1984), *Other Women*, Penguin Books, Harmondsworth, 1985 edn

—, *Bedrock*, Viking, Harmondsworth, 1990

—, *Five Minutes in Heaven*, Penguin Books, Harmondsworth, 1995

French, Marilyn (1977), *The Women's Room*, Sphere Books, London, 1979 edn

Piercy, Marge (1976), *Woman on the Edge of Time*, The Women's Press, London, 1979 edn

Other References

Kappeler, Susanne, *The Pornography of Representation*, Polity Press, Cambridge, 1986

Morris, Margaret Kissam, 'Lesbians in the Mainstream', review of *Five Minutes in Heaven*, *The Lesbian Review of Books*, 2, 2 (Winter 1995–6) pp23–4

LESBIAN WRITERS IN THE MAINSTREAM: SARA MAITLAND, JEANETTE WINTERSON AND EMMA DONOGHUE

Rachel Wingfield

Lesbians in the Mainstream before the Backlash

I am beginning with a contradiction. In a chapter on lesbians in mainstream publishing I am going to start with – and keep returning to – the work of Sara Maitland. Responses to this decision to date have ranged from 'Sara Maitland isn't a lesbian, is she?' to 'Sara Maitland, isn't she married to a vicar?'[1] Personally, I have no doubts at all about including Sara Maitland's writing in a discussion on lesbian fiction, for reasons which I hope will become apparent. Perhaps most contradictory – and interesting – of all is that I have chosen to write about Sara Maitland because as a lesbian feminist I find her work to be more radical, more inspiring and more political than many of the more publicly heralded lesbian authors. Sara Maitland would probably enjoy this contradiction herself – her own work is characterised by contradictions, doubts and uncertainties. But contradictions provide an opportunity, a key for looking at the assumptions which underlie them and the certainties which appear to prevail the rest of the time.

Sara Maitland's work began to be noticed and read by lesbian feminists in 1984, when *Virgin Territory* was published. At that time, Jeanette Winterson was yet to publish *Oranges Are Not The Only Fruit* and Emma Donoghue was still in high school. In 1984, the women's movement continued to ride on the wave of its strength and popularity in the 1970s. Beset by strife and divisions, it had still not received its crushing blow: the fundamental split which later took place around sexuality, and which focused on pornography and sado-masochism. Feminism hovered on the brink of this great divide, but a dialogue was still open.

This was the time I became a feminist; still at school, living in a small town, beginning to be an activist, I (amazingly) managed to discover feminist books in the local library. *Virgin Territory* was one of them – the first novel I had ever read which included lesbian feminist ideas. It had a profound impact on me, as I know it did on other women.

The prevailing mood within feminism then was that women (all women) were oppressed; violence against women, including pornography and sado-masochism, was a key means by which this oppression was both maintained and constructed. Heterosexuality was defined as a socially constructed institution for the first time – an institution which served the interests of male-dominated society, be it patriarchy, capitalism or some combination of the two, and which posited heterosexuality as the only acceptable form of sexuality. Debates raged over whether heterosexual practice was inevitably collusion and the idea that lesbianism could be a political choice was put forward. Feminism also identified the various forms of protection and privilege promised to those women who remained within heterosexual boundaries. On offer were two roles: good woman (virgin, wife, mother) or bad woman (prostitute, mistress, 'slag'). You could be either, you could even be both. But until you stepped outside of those categories altogether they were still defining you.

Virgin Territory is set firmly within the context of these debates. Its central character, Anna, is a nun sent to London by her religious order in South America because she has had a 'breakdown' following the rape of another nun, Sister Kitty. The rape has had a profound effect on Anna's psyche – she isn't sure of anything any more, and in particular she's not sure if she still wants to be a nun. Terrified of the void which may lie beneath all the certainties she has lived by until now, Anna is controlled and bullied by voices inside her head; voices of 'the fathers' who urge her to be a good nun, to submit to the authority of the patriarchal order and not to dare question it.

In London, Anna is faced with two possible alternatives to this order. One is in the form of her identification with a brain-damaged child, Caro, who represents the parts of Anna which she has always felt were unacceptable. Dirty, messy, out of control, not contained by any conventional boundaries, Caro is the 'bad girl' in Anna who existed before socialisation and who refused to submit to it. Anna projects Caro's voice, hearing it talking to her inside her own head, tempting and willing her to give up her connection to the outside world once and for all and to join her at the bottom of the pit before the boundaries which separated form, space and time existed.

Anna both fears and desires this void, but she realises that she does not want to enter it and never come out. The alternative to the order of the Fathers has to be more than simply dis-order: self-destruction is no rebellion. As the Fathers themselves say of Caro, 'Don't be deceived by her power. It is only anti-power. There is no power but the power of the Fathers. There is no other power' (p72). But there may be. The other alternative Anna finds in London is a lesbian feminist one which sees sisterhood as the positive power, a power which lies outside the patriarchal boundaries and challenges Anna's beliefs about religious celibacy. A chance meeting with Karen, a lesbian socialist feminist academic, gives Anna access to new ideas and a new way of understanding her virginity:

> Look at the archetypes; what have you got? You get the wife and mother, and the sex symbol and the friend-and-companion, and you get the virgin, all in this nice tidy balanced square, polarised, orderly, acceptable. But who's standing in the middle of the square? ... Men, that's who, they're doing the defining. And the virgin bit is ... a totally negative image: it's the power of not, of

not being owned by a man, of not relating sexually to a man ... If we want to talk about change and freedom we have to ... smash the square (p31–2).

And Karen knows how the square could be smashed: 'What's missing from the square, is the lesbian. And that's how we break it. The dyke is the positive image of the negative virgin' (p132). Karen's feminism also enables Anna to understand why the rape had such an impact on her: 'protection' for 'good women' within patriarchy is a con. Even nuns can be raped.

Virgin Territory is also set during the beginning of the debates around sado-masochism. Anna and Karen meet because Karen is researching the Church and women's masochism, studying some of the female saints and the admiration they gained through harming themselves. Masochism in the novel is set firmly within the context of male power, and the eroticisation of women's submission promoted by powerful institutions like the Roman Catholic Church throughout history. Anna's guilt and self-hatred are shown to inspire her own masochistic fantasies. Her masochism intensifies as she begins to acknowledge her sexual feelings for Karen; the voices in her head say she should be grateful for punishment which may save her from this 'perversion':

She craved it suddenly, physically, her belly melting, wanting, warming: greedy for her own humiliation, her own rape. Christ, she cried. She could not stay here in the church with her head full of such filth. 'Rape me chaste.' She begged God and the Fathers sneered; they would consider it, they told her, if she was very good. If she deserved it (pp52–3).

As some lesbians were beginning to argue that masochism was liberating for women, Maitland provides a clear, convincing analysis of women's masochism as originating in internalised hatred of women and their sexuality – the opposite to the celebratory passion for women espoused by Karen and the other lesbian feminists in *Virgin Territory*.

However, in an increasingly individualistic society – Thatcher was in power, proclaiming alongside the postmodernists that 'there is no such thing as society' – a liberal rather than feminist lesbian politics was to thrive. In 1985 Winterson's *Oranges Are Not The Only Fruit* was published to great acclaim, winning the Whitbread Award for First Novel. The book was able to be so successful in the mainstream because it was a beautiful, clever, original piece of work, but also because lesbian feminist politics and publications – including *Virgin Territory* – had laid the foundations. A discourse was in circulation which had already begun to question whether heterosexuality was the only acceptable option for women.

Little of this was apparent within the pages of the novel itself. Not a feminist idea, character or insight crosses the pages of *Oranges'* core narrative. There is no context for Jeanette's, the main character's, lesbianism, for her rebellion against her strict, fundamentalist upbringing, except for an 'anti-authority'/individualist one – precisely the one rejected by the lesbian feminists in *Virgin Territory*.

Clearly, Jeanette's story of growing up among Evangelists in a northern town is an authentic one. However, writing as an adult – as its narrator does – in the context of a vibrant women's movement, Winterson chooses to ignore its very existence. We see its influence only in the form which the author's very early foray into technical experimentalism takes. Alongside the central narrative in *Oranges*, Winterson retells the story in other forms. The female *Bildungsroman* is counterposed to traditional male narratives of mythical heroism in battle (the King Arthur legends) and to the language of fairy-tale magic. Lots of feminist authors were experimenting with rewriting patriarchal narratives at the time, and have since. Sara Maitland herself was doing it with Michelene Wandor, retelling the story of Noah in *Arky Types* (1987).

Set in a context of lesbian feminist theoretical debates,

as well as within a lesbian feminist reality, *Virgin Territory* offers a positive where *Oranges* and others before it had only a negative. The lesbians in *Virgin Territory* are imperfect, arrogant with it, and do not manage half of the time to cope with the contradictions of trying to live their politics within a patriarchal culture. None the less, they are bright, clear and present an alternative which is exciting, rebellious, warm and dangerous. Dangerous because it means losing the little protection that society affords women who remain within the parameters of male sexuality.

Into the 1990s: Feminism without Women; Sexuality without Gender

As we moved towards the 1990s the increasing influence of postmodernist theory and the individualist social and economic reforms which underlay it became evident. Queer politics swept through the lesbian community, reinforcing many of the dominant notions which had existed before the second wave of feminism. Butch/femme and sado-masochism were repackaged as liberating and radical. Feminist theory which saw loving women as involving a political and personal rebellion against patriarchy was replaced by arguments that sexuality was an individual preference that had nothing to do with politics. This backlash was matched within high theory by postmodernist attacks on any politics which still talked about power structures. As reality became simply a matter of subjective experience, and meaning became endlessly shifting, fixing any identity – lesbian or woman, for example – was viewed as old hat. For feminists this was a problem: how could women be oppressed if the category woman could not be said to exist? Where was feminism without women, and more to the point, where was lesbianism?

These theoretical developments can be traced through the novels of both these authors. Winterson, more individualist in her approach from the start, went with the flow of postmodernism with seemingly little trouble. The postmodernist preoccupation with writing about writing became more prominent in her later novels, until it seemed that the techniques became the end in themselves; the form not facilitating the communication of the content, but becoming all Winterson had to say instead of how she said it.

Written on the Body (1990) fixes Winterson most firmly within the mainstream literary community and its preoccupation with postmodernism. Winterson's audience is not intended to be feminists, lesbians or even the general public: it is the (male) mainstream literati itself. The 'experiment' around which *Written on the Body* revolves lies in the androgyny of its narrator. The reader is not allowed to know the gender of the narrator – who presumably is intended to be neither male nor female – nor their sexuality (s/he sleeps with both men and women, though mainly women). In true postmodernist fashion, gender and sexuality 'shift' throughout the novel as the reader constructs alternately the gender and sexuality of the narrator. The story of the novel, such as it is, focuses on the love affair between the narrator and a married woman, Louise, whom we later discover has cancer.

Although the novel clearly intends to explore all sorts of themes, including a key one of body as text versus body as biology, its technical experiment dominates all else. Rather than enhancing the work and challenging the reader, the narrator's lack of gender simply becomes an irritating ploy by which the author seems to be playing games with us. Winterson's skill in creating characters with whom we easily engage, a feature of her earlier work, immediately goes out the window. The narrator is impossible to engage with – an interesting enough finding in itself you may think – but the novel is never more than a series of experiments in form, with some rather beautiful, poetic prose to hold it together.

As a reader, I would love Winterson to allow some of her other skills to come to the fore again. Some of the writing in *Oranges* is simply stunning in its ability to fuse poetry and prose, to invoke pathos and to make us laugh.

Winterson can write about loss and betrayal like no one else. One of the strengths of her earlier writing is its authenticity, its eccentricity and its ability to express directly what it feels like to be on the outside. What perhaps made *Oranges* so popular were the humour, affection and detail with which its fine array of characters is drawn. Her reactive shift into an increasing focus on the theoretical concerns of the (male) literary world has meant that the experiences of lesbians, and women experiencing oppression generally, are written out of her work. The impact of class on women's lives, explored so powerfully in *Oranges*, is again absent from her later work.

While Winterson was developing those skills intended to impress the literary critics, Sara Maitland was fine-tuning hers. *Virgin Territory* never received the critical acclaim which *Oranges* did, not least because of its more radical politics. But there were other reasons. In many ways it plays *Wuthering Heights* to Winterson's *Jane Eyre* – like its central character, *Virgin Territory* is raw and uncontained. Reading it is an intense experience: it asks us to enter into the world of someone who hovers on the boundary between sanity and madness, who is holding on by the skin of her teeth, peering down into a bottomless chasm. The world she inhabits is a violent, passionate, frightening one where the options are very stark: you either fight back, you collude or you self-destruct. In later novels, Maitland returns to these themes, but the novels seem more able to contain their ambivalence. They are easier to read.

The characters in *Three Times Table* (1990) face many of the same dilemmas as Anna in *Virgin Territory*, including having to abandon the certainties and fantasies they have chosen to live by. *Three Times Table* explores male theories of knowledge – including evolution and theoretical physics – demonstrating their role as patriarchal narratives and there-fore social constructs, and takes a hard look at the implications and limitations for women of living with the reality of their influence. Here again, Maitland is grappling with positive and negative solutions to pain – self-destruction versus taking control and moving on. All three women in this novel – mother, daughter and granddaughter – know they have to face the future by confronting it. Although the influence of postmodernist thinking is apparent, Maitland as ever manages to hold the contradictions she invokes. While understanding uncertainty to be at the core of living, she also suggests that we have to act on the world despite that. Significantly, she concludes with lesbianism as the hope for the future of the next generation of women. In the context of such doubt, fifteen-year-old Maggie finds some certainty. When Maggie is called a 'dyke' by a gang of boys who have seen her in her friend Hermione's arms, Hermione responds by laughing and shouting to the boys:

> 'Don't worry...it's probably just a phase we're going through.'
> 'It's all right,' says Maggie, perfectly clear, her bell sounding again uncracked and certain as she had feared it never would. 'My grandmother says that a normal evolutionary phase can last two hundred million years' (p215).

Clare in *Home Truths* (1993) undergoes a similar journey while suffering from amnesia following an accident in which she lost her hand and her lover, David. Clare never remembers what happened to David, and in true postmodernist fashion Maitland avoids closure here, offering us possible explanations – a natural, biological one, a political one and a spiritual or magical one. Alternatively, Clare may have killed him. He was controlling and abusive and she certainly wanted to.

Home Truths is perhaps the most contradictory of Maitland's novels. On the one hand, the influence of post-modernism and queer politics is apparent in both its form and its content. We even have a gay sado-masochistic vicar caught out by the tabloids, and endeavouring to convince us that gay sado-masochism is risk-taking and daring, as opposed to the straight sado-masochism between Clare and David, which is portrayed as both destructive and stultifying. None the less, Maitland's own uncertainty and contradictions do not allow this trend in the narrative to dominate – whatever the conscious intention. *Home Truths* remains a lesbian feminist narrative at heart, surrounded though it is by seeming uncertainty. All her life Clare had run from risk and danger. During the course of the novel, she is able to confront and not flinch from her feelings for another woman. Psychically and literally, she moves from hiding in the safety of controlling heterosexuality, towards reclaiming the lesbian passion she ran from. She completes the journey Anna, in *Virgin Territory*, was not able to.

While Winterson retreated from lesbianism in her work, Maitland tells us again and again that lesbianism is the answer. One may argue that it is easier for her to get away with doing so in a mainstream press because everyone thinks of her as a vicar's wife. Perhaps Winterson feels more impelled to hide behind layers of masks because she is known to be a lesbian and now publishes with mainstream houses. However, Emma Donoghue, an Irish lesbian published by Penguin, seems to have been able to do so without either of these defences. The work that Maitland and Winterson, among others, did as forerunners has obviously partly enabled this to happen; Donoghue has got away with a lot more, a lot sooner in the mainstream.

Donoghue's novels, *Stir Fry* and *Hood*, published respectively in 1994 and 1995, provide an interesting comparison with the novels being published by Maitland and Winterson during these years. Unlike Winterson, Donoghue does not find it necessary to avoid either her gender or her sexuality to appeal to the mainstream, although she too has certainly been influenced by the backlash against feminism. Indeed, Donoghue seems altogether a lot less self-conscious about lesbianism than either Winterson or Maitland, with both positive and negative results. In *Stir Fry*, we read about one young woman's journey towards lesbianism, a theme we meet in *Oranges* and Maitland's novels generally. But Mariah's journey seems to have very little to do with rebellion against anything, be it patriarchy, or convention; and still less to do with a positive choice based on a passion for women and a desire to maintain her own integrity.

Mariah's 'decision' to become a lesbian does, however, have everything to do with uncovering her own desire for her two flatmates, Jael and Ruth, with whom she shares an extremely voyeuristic relationship. Away from home for the first time, at university in Dublin, Mariah falls half in love with both of them, only to be shocked to discover they are lesbians when she sees them kissing one evening.

Jael and Ruth provide two different models of lesbianism for Mariah. Ruth is a feminist who would like to have a relationship premised on equality, who is committed to her relationship with Jael and to her politics. Much more of a postmodernist invention, committed to neither lesbianism nor Ruth, Jael has no fixed sexual identity and finds politics boring. Mariah is attracted to Jael, but it is Ruth she chooses.

However, despite the inclusion of a lesbian feminist among the central characters – and even a women's-group meeting – feminism seems oddly peripheral to the novel. Ruth's lesbianism seems somehow separate from her feminism – the two never really connect – and there is no articulation of lesbian feminist ideas anywhere in the novel. It is interesting that although the women's movement in Ireland has a different history from that in Britain, the context presented in the novel is very similar to that of the women's movement in Britain. This may in part be due to the fact that Donoghue was living in Cambridge when the novel was written. Lesbian feminism is almost a backdrop, which in many ways it would have been for women of Mariah's generation. The legacy of the women's movement lingers on: the university still has a women's group, still has lesbians in it, but the group seems to exist more as part of a lifestyle than as a tool for changing the world.

In *Hood* this is even more apparent. The central characters are part of a lesbian feminist community – a far cry from anything either Maitland or Winterson was publishing at this stage – but somehow the distinction between this and any other kind of feminism, or indeed some kinds of heterosexuality, remains unclear. And while *Stir Fry* in its own way presents lesbianism as an enticing option, and quite cleverly unpacks Mariah's attempts to convince herself that she is heterosexual, *Hood*, despite its many attempts at portraying erotic lesbian sex – pages and pages – ultimately presents us yet again with an image of lesbian relationships as romantically tragic, and doomed to failure, as seen with Jael and Ruth's relationship in *Stir Fry*.

It is interesting to note that not one of these three novelists depicts any lasting, positive lesbian relationship for her protagonists. Those early representations of doomed, unhappy lesbians (a teacher of mine once said to me, 'I've got nothing against gays but they do seem to be very unhappy people, and they always make each other unhappy') lurk between the pages of our mainstream lesbian writers like ghosts, refusing to be expelled, outliving the growth of and backlash against the women's movement, moving into the 1990s with the message that maybe you can't ever trust a woman…

The Present Impasse: Of Mothers, Lovers, Loss and Betrayal

Having begun with one contradiction, I'm going to finish with another, and perhaps more than one.

All three authors have been seen as important in bringing the fictional representation of lesbians into the mainstream, and Winterson in particular has been regarded as a significant figure for many women coming to lesbianism for the first time. Yet even at the points in their literary career when they have been positive about the *idea* of lesbianism, none of these authors seems able to represent lesbian *relationships* in a positive light. Their representations of lesbian relationships are deeply embedded in the traditional patriarchal narratives of lesbian lives which have preceded them. From Colette to Radclyffe Hall, lesbian fiction writers have a tradition of portraying lesbian relationships in a manner consistent with dominant ideas on gender and sexuality. Sad, doomed from the start, passionate but filled with pain, romantic but tragic, we meet again in these novels the stories of our foresisters' fictional (and sometimes real) failures to build sustainable lesbian relationships.

So why has the passing of nearly a century and two waves of feminism had so little impact on even the way lesbians choose to portray their own relationships? One of the dominant lesbian discourses during this period has been a lesbian feminist one. Yet, even back in the mid-1980s, it is possible to see a deep ambivalence about relationships between women in both Winterson's and Maitland's fiction.

All three authors link the ambivalence their characters demonstrate in their adult relationships with women to feeling abandoned by, betrayed by or unable to separate from their mothers. As Adrienne Rich writes, our history as women in patriarchal culture has inevitably partially been one of betraying and lying to one another (Rich, pp 188–9). Our first relationship with a woman – our mother – may be fraught with contradictions in a world which pressurises mothers to collude with women's oppression and prepare their daughters to be 'good women'. We see the legacy of this history represented perhaps most clearly and forcefully in Winterson's work. *Oranges* is a very woman-centred world; men seem barely to exist. Men are 'the other', the beasts, and 'beasts are crafty' (p71). The impact of this, however, is not to present a positive image of the bonds between women in the absence of men. Quite the contrary. Jeanette is betrayed by one woman after another – her lover, Melanie; her ally in the Church, an older woman who uses Jeanette's vulnerability as an opportunity to get her into bed; and, most significantly, her mother. Her one friend, Elsie, dies and leaves her just when she needs her most. Jeanette's father is emotionally absent throughout the novel, and barely referred to – so much so that she tells Melanie when they first meet that she doesn't have a father.

The impact of Jeanette's mother's betrayal overshadows all others. On discovering her lesbianism, Jeanette's mother hands her over to Pastor Spratt of their Evangelical church and has her 'exorcised'. Afterwards she destroys all mementoes of Jeanette's relationship with Melanie:

> While I lay shivering in the parlour she took a tooth-comb to my room and found all the letters, all the cards, all the jottings of my own, and burnt them one night in the backyard. There are different sorts of treachery, but betrayal is betrayal wherever you find it. She burnt a lot more than the letters that night in the backyard. I don't think she knew. In her head she was still queen, but not my queen anymore, not the White Queen anymore (p109).

Later, finding this hasn't done the trick, Jeanette's mother throws her out. From being her mother's 'joy' in this close, strong, rather enmeshed bond, Jeanette is abandoned by her, first emotionally and then physically. Reflecting as an adult on her inability to trust the women she gets involved with, Jeanette again returns to the emotional language of her mother's betrayal for an explanation:

> One thing I am certain of, I do not want to be betrayed, but that's quite hard to say casually at the beginning of a relationship. It's not a word people use very often, which confuses me because there are different kinds of fidelity but betrayal is betrayal wherever you find it. By betrayal, I mean promising to be on your side, then being on someone else's (p165).

The material patriarchal world behind the misogynist world of the Evangelist church in *Oranges* barely gets a look in, other than in the form of Pastor Spratt. The emotionally female-dominated world of the narrator is so strong that the material power of male reality does not seem significant. It is no wonder, then, that the narrator does not turn to feminism as a way of understanding her life.

Terror of loss and betrayal continue to haunt Winterson's later work, particularly *Written on the Body*, in which the elusive Louise threatens the ultimate abandonment: death through cancer. What the narrator of this novel is forced to recognise, however, is that loss is the potential risk in any love and that risk is worth taking. 'It was worth it,' s/he realises. 'Love is worth it' (p156).

In a moment of insight the narrator recognises the fundamental flaw at the heart of the 'romance' of the doomed lesbian tragedies and finally tries to let go of them. Love itself – not the dramatics – is the challenge: 'What were my heroics and sacrifices really about? . . . Operatic heroics and a tragic end? What about a wasteful end?' (p187).

Yet the ambivalence remains. The relationship which is finally worth risking loss for can still slip through the net. It may not even be between two women.

Emma Donoghue similarly focuses on themes of betrayal and loss in *Hood*. Pen's lover, Cara, has died, yet the pain she begins to experience after her death is for the losses she underwent before Cara died. Pen begins to ask herself whether she had in fact lost Cara a long time before her death. And whether Cara was emotionally absent from their relationship from the start.

The novel begins with a flashback: Pen remembers an incident in which she and Cara were out shopping one day and Cara suddenly, unpredictably, runs away from her. Cara never offers any explanation for this behaviour, but the impression given to the reader is that Cara felt a sudden bout of claustrophobia, an urge to escape; that somehow the bonds of this relationship were too tight. Cara was abandoned by her mother as a child and as an adult felt trapped by Pen's presence, but panicked at the thought of losing her. In her relationship with Cara, Pen re-experienced what happened with her own mother, who also had sudden bouts of 'claustrophobia', wishing to escape the needs and proximity of her children, who were so attached to her. Cara has sexual relationships with other women; Pen does not. Cara endeavours to persuade Pen that this is no betrayal, quoting Jeanette's line from *Oranges*: 'By betrayal I mean promising to be on your side and then being on someone else's.' She tells Pen, 'I'm always on your side' (p215), and Pen does believe her. But the child in Pen who always felt at risk of abandonment recalls:

> Sometimes when I was alone in the big house at night and the wind made the panes rattle, I forgot the explanations and I was 3 years old. My mother once said the worst thing about having children was that when she went into the cubicle of a public toilet, we would begin to snivel, and while she was struggling with her zip she would see these little hands come under the door, and would get an overpowering urge to stamp on them. I could understand that, but I could also understand the abased neediness that motivated Gavin and me to put our hands under the door (p215).

Like Pen's mother, Cara runs from feeling overwhelmed by Pen's needs. Pen can no more give up hope of having those needs met one day by Cara than she could of having them met by her mother. Especially as Cara occasionally seems to offer that promise of fulfilment.

Pen and Cara lived double lives: in the closet to their family and their workmates, but known as lovers in the lesbian feminist community. Forced to hide behind masks, they also hid from each other. As Adrienne Rich writes, in a comment particularly pertinent to lesbians in a heterosexist society, 'In the struggle to survive we are forced to tell lies, but the risk run by the liar is that she will forget she is lying' (Rich, p189). The risk, from Rich's point of view, is that the liar will thus become alienated from herself and those with whom she tries to be intimate. The cost of Cara and Pen's closet life was immense but unrecognised by them, and becomes apparent only when Cara dies and Pen is unable to share her grief with colleagues or family. Yet the novel raises a complex question here. Were Pen and Cara forced to hide behind masks because of fear of reprisal, or was this life in the closet chosen by them as an evasion of risk, because they both had a history in which intimacy – being one's true self with another – was to be feared anyway? Did the closet provide a convenient means by which to avoid having to dismantle barriers, particularly with parents?

The conclusion of the novel, and the point at which Pen eventually cries, is when she decides finally to try having an open, honest conversation with her mother for the first time in her life. *Hood* closes with Pen sitting at her mother's kitchen table, about to tell her she's a lesbian, prepared to acknowledge that the child within her still needs her mother: 'This birth is long overdue, mother. It'll be a tight squeeze. You'd better open your arms to this screaming red bundle, because it's the only one I'll ever bring you' (p309).

All of Sara Maitland's protagonists are preoccupied with mothers, and their current relationships with women are complicated by this preoccupation. Anna in *Virgin Territory* was, like Cara and Jeanette, abandoned by her mother. Anna's mother left her to be brought up by her father, who expected her to be the adult. When she meets Karen, the 'bad girl' inside her feels she may have found a mother at last. The longing to be held, to be given a hot bath and wrapped up, is finally met by Karen, and therein lies the confusion because Karen is offering lesbian feminism and adult sexuality. What Anna emotionally wants is a mother and Karen can never be that. Realising in the end that Karen cannot save her, cannot take responsibility for her, Anna goes her own way. She cannot trust herself with Karen, because she does not feel adult enough to meet her on equal terms. But this means the novel is left open. We are not entirely sure if lesbian feminism is the path Anna will take, for what she was looking for from it was an experience from other women which could somehow put right and heal the loss and betrayal of women in the past. As she herself realises, she is currently confusing her feelings about her mother with those towards the women close to her now: 'Until she found her mother, she could not love her sisters because she could not tell who they were' (p231).

Anna does not allow herself to express her anger and ambivalence with women in general and mothers in particular until the end of the novel. Even then she projects the anger, hearing in her mind the voice of Caro expressing her anger with her own mother for abandoning her as a child:

> You blame the Fathers but I have to ask, where are the mothers then? ... The mothers desert the daughters. They sell us to the Fathers, over and over again ... They are busy gnawing through the cord so they can sell us off, and their price is cheap. I hate them. I hate them. They go away. They ought to stay with the daughters but they go away (p218).

In the novels discussed here, we find an array of angry, wounded, motherless daughters, abandoned or betrayed as children – Jeanette, Anna, Cara, Clare in *Home Truths* – alongside characters like Pen and the three generations in *Three Times Table*, battling out the complex process of trying to separate from and at the same time maintain their attachment to their mothers. Both abandonment and engulfment are equally feared – Clare, for example, has two mothers, one representing each of these fears. The security a mother may provide is also a constraint. Jeanette in *Oranges* sums this up when she talks ambivalently of her attachment to her mother, still as strong years after her mother has thrown her out: 'She had tied a thread around my button, to tug when she pleased' (p171).

Conclusion
The ambivalence that Maitland, Winterson and Donoghue leave us with in their novels reflects the process that has taken place within lesbian feminism itself in recent years.

Disillusionment with the possibility of sisterhood, its failure to meet impossible emotional expectations, has bitterly impacted on the movement.[2] (A consequent idealisation of 'bad' women – dangerous, cruel, violent or just plain cold and hard – has been the result.) Proponents of queer theory and postmodernism were able to benefit from this disjuncture. The work of all three authors reflects the influence of postmodernist discourse on sexuality and the concurrent backlash against feminism. Of the three, Maitland is the most influenced by, and in dialogue with, lesbian feminist ideas although she is not considered to be a 'lesbian author'.

All three of these authors have made it to the mainstream perhaps partly because their novels represent lesbian relationships in ambivalent forms, in contrast to more unreservedly feminist or idealised representations. None of the authors involves her protagonists in even mildly contented lesbian relationships. There are hopes for the future for characters like Mariah, Pen, Anna and Clare, but there are no representations of happy lesbian lovers in these novels.

Jeanette in *Oranges* voices her disappointed expectations: 'The unknownness of my needs frightens me, I do not know how huge they are or how high they are, I only know they are not being met' (p165). All of these characters struggle with the question of how to form attachments with adult women, to take that risk having defended themselves alone for so long. The voices in the texts seem to beg the question, is it worth even trying to build new models of relating to women, in which fear of intimacy and betrayal do not dominate? Or are lesbians after all doomed – in our self-representations – to repeat the dramas, tragedies and failures of our foresisters?

These novels remind us that many women do not enter lesbianism loving women, or even liking them much, although the bonds they feel with other women may be strong. In this context, lesbian feminism has to struggle with many more impelling, more mainstream narratives, which offer solutions that can appear to be less threatening, less demanding and a good deal more romantic.

REFERENCES

Novels

Donoghue, Emma (1994), *Stir Fry*, Penguin Books, Harmondsworth, 1995 edn

—, *Hood*, Hamish Hamilton, Harmondsworth, 1995

Maitland, Sara (1984), *Virgin Territory*, Pavanne, London, 1995 edn

—, *Three Times Table*, Chatto and Windus, London, 1990

—, *Home Truths*, Chatto and Windus, London, 1993

Wandor, Michelene and Sara Maitland, *Arky Types*, Methuen, London, 1987

Winterson, Jeanette (1985), *Oranges Are Not The Only Fruit*, Vintage, London, 1991 edn

— (1990), *Written on the Body*, Jonathan Cape, London, 1992 edn

Other References

Maitland, Sara, *A Book of Spells*, Michael Joseph, Harmondsworth, 1987

Rich, Adrienne (1975), 'Women and Honor. Some Notes on Lying', in *On Lies, Secrets and Silence: Selected Prose*, W. W. Norton and Company, New York and London, 1995 edn

NOTES

1 See Sara Maitland's own account of dealing with these responses in her collection *A Book of Spells* (1987).

2 This deep ambivalence about relations between women is rather serious for a political force dependent on 'sisterhood' for its success. Lesbian feminism in particular, unlike lesbianism *per se*, has at its base a belief in a commitment to women, a vision of lesbianism as a choice to positively celebrate and value our own, who have been so hated and violated throughout the centuries. In the face of patriarchy's attempts to encourage women to mistrust one

another and to battle over men, lesbian feminism argues that we can defeat patriarchy by uniting against it. Looking back to our mothers, we can rediscover the women who have been made invisible by patriarchal narratives and rewrite our own, reclaiming the bonds between women and the struggles they fought as they did so.

LINDSAY GORDON MEETS KATE BRANNIGAN — MAINSTREAMING OR MALESTREAMING: REPRESENTATIONS OF WOMEN CRIME FIGHTERS

Jill Radford

In this chapter I will be taking a stroll through the crime novels or detective fiction stories[1] of one of my favourite UK writers, Val McDermid. After a brief introduction to her work, my aim is to speculate on the appeal of her lesbian detective books featuring Lindsay Gordon, and to consider her later and more mainstream stories with heterosexual private investigator (PI) Kate Brannigan. I contrast these two sleuths, the stories they inhabit and conclude with a discussion of mainstreaming lesbian/ lesbian feminist writing.

Reading fiction is a bit more complex than it seems. The meaning of stories is defined primarily by the author, but is mediated by the genre and processes of its production, and importantly by the readers. These constitutive elements of meaning are shaped by the wider social, political and cultural context, including patriarchy, racism and economic structures, particularly those of the publishing industry. In contrast, postmodernist literary criticism claims that readings of texts are so multiple or personalised that no one, not even the author, has any privileged authority. Rather, in a Humpty Dumpty world, words or texts mean what we want them to and no one can challenge any reading. As is now increasingly recognised, postmodernism has claimed for itself a sound feminist insight and then rendered it meaningless through exaggerated relativism.

The Genre

Val McDermid's work has been seen as part of a new wave of feminist and/or lesbian crime fiction. As Linda Semple (undated) has pointed out, this fiction is part of the wider boom in feminist literature, but also links back to an earlier genre of women's thriller writing, retaining and sometimes subverting aspects of this tradition. It has often been argued that, while populated by strong and inventive female detectives, the classic tradition of women's thriller writing is a conservative one. A common scenario is that of a comfortable social world disrupted by a criminal outrage; enter the detective who follows clues and herrings and names the villain; order is restored and good wins over evil. Lesbian and most feminist thrillers adopt similar conventions but subvert or transform them. As I will illustrate, it is this which in part makes for their radicalism. The commitment to securing justice for women, wronged either by the police and criminal justice system or by male violence, is another aspect of their radicalism.

Val McDermid has produced two series of detective stories: the Lindsay Gordon books – *Report for Murder* (1987), *Common Murder* (1989), *Final Edition* (1991), *Union Jack* (1993); and *Booked for Murder* (1996) – and the Kate Brannigan series – *Dead Beat* (1992), *Kick Back* (1993), *Crack Down* (1994), *Clean Break* (1995) and *Blue Genes* (1996).[2] Both demonstrate that she has mistressed the craft of producing cracking good stories – exciting, fast moving – with complex interwoven plots and subplots to baffle the reader, and even at times the intrepid detectives, who nevertheless confound the cops and reveal the true villain, thereby putting the world to rights. The sheroes in both series are strong women, tough, persistent and streetwise, impressing with their courage and ability to survive serious danger. They are gifted with positive talents: acute observational power, astute logic and sensitive insight, the skills to enable them to get out of tricky situations, physical stamina, the ability to 'charm the hind leg off a donkey' and crack the case by writing lists, collecting clues and gossiping round the networks. They can resolve murders and still have fun.

Lindsay Gordon is a lesbian, feminist and socialist who earns her living from journalism. She is drawn into the part of amateur sleuth by friends who have an unfortunate habit of getting in the way of murders and appealing for help. This puts her in an outsider/insider role in relation to the investigation. In contrast, Kate Brannigan is a private eye, a partner in a firm of investigators, though this does not stop her taking on the odd case for a friend. Consequently, she approaches the investigation as more of an outsider, albeit with good connections. Differences between our sheroes, their sexuality and their levels of commitment to their cases, make for their distinctiveness. Lindsay Gordon is called on to investigate happenings in the world she knows but never where she's actually living, the worlds of feminism, socialism and lesbian networks. These worlds form the political context and backgrounds to her stories. Kate Brannigan, PI, occupies a different space. She investigates on behalf of clients and their stories take her into diverse worlds or underworlds. These differences are more blurred in *Blue Genes*, the fifth in the Kate Brannigan series, where Kate ends up acting for friends and breaching the PI professional code. With this qualification, the outsider status of PI confines these stories to the women's crime writing conventions. Kate is called on to deal with the crime and to restore the world to its previous order. In contrast, in the Lindsay Gordon books, it is Lindsay's standpoint, as a lesbian socialist feminist, insider and friend, that makes the books far more radical as the disrupted order is defined from a lesbian standpoint. Further, the endings are more complicated as the order is never fully restored, since the costs of crime are portrayed as more far-reaching.

Locating lesbian detective novels within the wider genre, Magda Devas points out, 'The lesbian detective gets her cred in much the same way as her male colleague by performing astonishing feats of courage and deduction, and by simply being the Goodie. The lesbian heroine need only add a commitment to women, and/or lesbian feminism, and she is off and away' (Devas, p28).

The appeal of these books, for me, works at many levels and includes the thrill of thrillers, the puzzles of detection; an insider's representation of the challenges and delights of lesbian friendship networks, and the ups and downs of feminist politics and praxis. The fun of playing lesbian games with the rules of the detective genre, the political context and affirmation of strong lesbian identities are some of the reasons I always look forward to the next book. Devas explores the interesting idea of the lesbian detective as having a magical quality. This may explain how Lindsay Gordon can routinely survive bereavements, betrayals, physical violence and exile while building a sound career and finding love in ways which seem astounding, as well as the power accorded to both sleuths in solving crimes and determining the fates of major players at the conclusion of the novels.

A particular appeal lies in the power of both detectives to reach the truth traditional law enforcement cannot reach. For me, as a long-time campaigner working on women's relation to law and criminal justice, sharing the bettering of patriarchal plod is a definite plus. These victories are achieved in part by the superiority of the 'big purple cells', as opposed to 'little grey ones' – that is, women's superior use of logic and also 'feminine intuition', or actually hearing what is said. Success also stems from the women's better networks, be they feminist and lesbian communities, the music industry, the art world or the worlds of small-time builders and estate agents. Commitment to the case, the autonomy arising from their not being part of the police and quirks of coincidence or magic which never happen in the real world all play a part.

Val McDermid, in conversation with Libby Brooks, identifies women's growing dissatisfaction with and distrust of law enforcement agencies and the legal system as a reason why modern-day women detectives tend to be PIs or amateurs free to act according to their own moralities, rather than belonging to the force. She goes on to say, 'It's hard to imagine a woman crime writer of my generation creating the likes of Wexford or Dalgleish. The public in general no longer has confidence in the police. Women are even more dissatisfied because there is this extra element of not just being perceived as criminal, but as "bad women"' (Brooks, p12).

Part of the radicalism of the stories turns on this autonomy. The sleuths can act, think and reflect independently, and in doing so promote values and world views informed by feminist and lesbian politics and ethics. Nevertheless, Val McDermid doesn't write off policewomen as potential allies of the feminist crime fighter, any more than a wise activist does. It is interesting perhaps that it is Kate Brannigan, PI, rather than Lindsay Gordon, socialist, feminist and lesbian, who develops a strategic friendship with a woman police officer who smoothes out her dealings with the boys in blue, leaving Lindsay, alone or with a friend, to struggle against the prejudices of the force.

Val McDermid also uses the moral autonomy of the independent feminist sleuth to present readers with intriguing and contemporary ethical dilemmas, illustrating the ways the narratives pick up on current debates in lesbian and feminist communities. For example, in *Blue Genes*, one storyline engages with controversies stemming from the potential of the new reproductive technology and assisted pregnancy services. Should heterosexual PI Kate Brannigan tell a pregnant lesbian mother that she may not be the biological mother of the child she's carrying or, even worse, that it might be the biological child of a woman bad beyond belief. Does the sleuth have the wisdom as well as the power of the goddess to resolve these conundrums or are they more properly matters for the collective?

Other dilemmas arise when the villain of the piece turns out to be a lesbian. How does the pc PI deal with a fictional lesbian killer? Should she hand her over to the forces of law and patriarchal order or give her time to exile herself? Does it make a difference if the lesbian is responsible for the death of another woman, and if that woman is also a lesbian or even a former lover? Does it matter if she was provoked or acting in self-preservation? These questions are drawn from narratives in both series and link to contemporary struggles about women's relationship to (in)justice in the real world. As I will discuss later, these storylines also raise prior questions about the construction of lesbians as evil, but the question here is how that evil is dealt with. Val McDermid accords the power to resolve such dilemmas to the sleuths alone. If a lesbian villain is allowed to escape, is this ending a radical subversion of the traditional thriller or simply one more comfortable for a lesbian author and her lesbian readership?

Women's reasons for dissatisfaction with policing and the criminal justice system turn on issues of sexism, racism and a long history of police failure to respond appropriately to women victimised by male violence and double standards which inform responses to women as perpetrators of crime. These are some of the issues specifically explored in the storylines which also address the consequences of crime: imprisonment or exile on the one side and victimisation and disruption on the other. Val McDermid engages with these perennial themes of crime writing in terms of what they mean for women and for lesbians particularly. One recurrent theme, for example, is the impact of imprisonment on women: 'Already life behind bars had left its mark on her. Her skin had an unhealthy sallowness. There were dark bags beneath her eyes. But what was most striking was that she seemed to have lost all her self-confidence. Fewer than three days of living behind bars had cut her down to less than life-size' (*Report for Murder*, p98).

As well as righting the wrongs of the police and criminal justice system so that 'good' wins out and the innocent go free, feminist detective fiction is also about securing justice for women. This can entail rescuing the wrongfully suspected or convicted woman, or bringing a culprit to justice for wrongs committed against women, or indeed both. Having been involved in feminist campaigns, I know it is a long slog, requiring the concerted effort of many women, to secure justice for individual women, like Kiranjit Ahluwalia or Emma Humphreys.[3] It takes even longer, if indeed it is possible, to make those fundamental transformations of law and criminal justice needed to create a situation in which women can expect justice as of right. Until that time, there's a sweetness in feminist sleuths outdoing the forces of law and order. The speed with which our sheroes put things right is fantastic. Obvious differences exist between fighting for justice for women in the real world and in fantasy. For a start, fictional detectives, in line with the traditions of the genre, are called on as non-accountable individuals, although this convention is subverted to a degree. Lindsay Gordon is not a complete loner. She has friendship networks and lovers to talk things through with, so making the detective process a more collaborative and more feminist one. These women also take responsibility for healing wounds and nurturing the shero back to health and strength. Kate Brannigan also has a network of friends, but they are a mixed bunch who create as many problems as they solve.

The fictional detective holds power over the cast of players. These powers can be used to right wrongs against women, together with a well-aimed Thai-boxing kick, a carefully planned stake-out, a bit of computer hacking and the shadowing of suspects' cars through urban jungles. The feminist magician also holds the fate of the villains in her hands at the conclusion of the novel, and in at least two novels this power is also used to the advantage of lesbian villains.

Intrepid Dykes

The storylines of the Lindsay Gordon mysteries are grounded in the feminist and lesbian communities of the period. The stories are linked through the character of Lindsay and some of her friends and lovers. Following her life, from freelance Scottish journalist grieving for a lover who died from cancer, through new loves and new jobs, to becoming an academic living by a beach in California, is one appeal of the books.

Common Murder provides the clearest expression of feminist politics and practice. It is set in a women's peace camp at the gates of fictional Brownlow Common US air base and is clearly an insider's representation of Greenham. *Report for Murder* and *Final Edition* convincingly portray feminist and lesbian networks in Glasgow and London. Val McDermid's own socialist roots are perhaps most visible in *Union Jack*, set in the 1990s at a trade union conference, described with the confidence and humour of someone familiar with those scenarios. In these books it is the settings and perspectives attributed to the characters which create their political frameworks. Both *Common Murder* and *Union Jack* present insider accounts of political struggles, mildly sending up political process and practice, sometimes in very funny ways, but from an overall standpoint of shared politics. In *Union Jack*, each chapter opens with witty snippets from 'Advice for New Delegates' a Standing Orders Sub-Committee booklet, which invites us to share a giggle at the antics of the boys. In *Common Murder*, we learn that the women's peace camp provided Lindsay 'with a focus for her flagging political energies and...she enjoyed the company of the peace women...Brownlow Common had become one of Lindsay's favourite boltholes' (p5).

Lindsay takes comfort from, as well as giving support to, the peace camp. However, Val McDermid also allows her to behave badly, to poke fun at lesbian and feminist politics and ethics, in ways that are not always welcomed by campaigners as the following interchange on vegetarianism illustrates:

The child nodded. 'What are we having for breakfast? Have you brought bacon and eggs like you promised last time?'

'I managed to smuggle them past the vegetarian checkpoint on the way in,' Lindsay joked. 'I know you're

like me, Cara, you love the things everyone tells you are
bad for you' (p25).

Here, Lindsay is able to make the kind of comment, and
to a child, which in other circumstances would be close to
the stereotyped press attacks on peace women as
doctrinaire and neglectful as mothers. Also in relation to
political process, she voices clichéd criticism about
collective meetings and decision-making, although this
criticism is mediated by the fact of her participation:

Lindsay still couldn't get used to the way they struggled
to avoid hierarchies by refusing to run their meetings
according to traditional structures. Instead they sat in a
big circle and each spoke in turn, supposedly without
interruption (p28).

They made their way back to the camp, where the adults
settled down in the meeting bender for a long session.
Three hours later, it had been agreed that the women
charged the day before should, if they were willing, opt
for prison for the sake of publicity...It had been a
stormy meeting and Lindsay was glad when it was over.
Even though she had by now experienced many of these
talking shops, she never failed to become slightly
disillusioned at the destructive way women could fight
against each other in spite of their common cause (p32).

In these illustrations, the author relies on a shared
political perspective with her readers. Lindsay gets away
with the criticisms because her underlying support is
recognised by the intended readership. These same
comments read by those hostile to the politics would take
on a very different meaning.

Although *Common Murder* and *Union Jack* are politically grounded stories, Val McDermid has said she does
not use the stories to promote any narrow political agenda
or allow the characters to rant: 'The politics underpins
what I am writing and emerge as part of the story. I don't

start with the issues – I want them to emerge as a natural organic part of the book. My characters may express strong opinions but I don't think I preach' (Brooks, p13).

Val McDermid may not preach, but Lindsay Gordon certainly creates waves over class. For example, *Report for Murder*, set in a girls' public (private) school provides the opportunity for critical reflection on class privilege. On hearing details of the school's financial crisis and being asked to be sympathetic in her coverage of a fund-raising event, Lindsay expresses ambivalence:

'I can't help feeling it wouldn't be such a bad thing if the public schools felt the pinch like everyone else. It seems somewhat unreal to be worrying about playing fields when a lot of state schools can't even afford the books to go round...

'What about all the kids in exactly the same boat who don't have the benefit of Mummies and Daddies with enough spare cash to use Derbyshire House as a social services department? Maybe their lives would be a little better if the middle classes had to opt back into real life and use their influence to improve things. I can't be anything but totally opposed to this system you so cheerfully shore up' (pp8, 9).

Pragmatism rules and Lindsay accepts the commission and subsequently works to save the school by solving the murder which threatened to bring it into disrepute. Contradictions around class continue to trouble Lindsay throughout this story. Most crucially they come close to jeopardising her relationship with Cordelia Brown. Her first visit to Cordelia's home overlooking Highbury Fields in London leads to just one of the several clashes over class which characterise their partnership:

Cordelia caught sight of Lindsay's expression and grinned.

'Don't worry,' she said, 'it's not as grand as it looks. My accountant told me that property was the best investment, so I lashed out on this with proceeds of my early success in the mass media...

'Well, to be fair, it's not all the proceeds of my sweated labour. My grandmother died three years ago and left me a rather large legacy. That went on the deposit for this place. Most of the rest of the money has come from telly, radio and the film I scripted last year...'

'You really are one of the obscenely privileged minority, aren't you', remarked Lindsay ... 'In my job, I see so much poverty, so much deprivation, so much exploitation, I can't help feeling luxury like this is obscene. Don't you want to change things?'

Cordelia laughed and replied lightly, 'But what would you have me do? Give all I have to the poor?'

Lindsay saw the chasm yawning at her feet. She could leave the argument lying for a future day when there might be a strong enough relationship between them to stand the weight of disagreement. Or she could pursue the subject relentlessly and kill the magic stone dead... (p108).

I have quoted this passage at some length because it is interesting at several levels. It not only points to the place of class in Lindsay's socialist feminism. It also highlights the centrality of identity politics in the 1980s lesbian community, and the issues of inequality, and dealing with inequality, in lesbian relationships, points of tension around which little has been written.[4] Class resurfaces through the series. The fifth novel finds Lindsay with her lover in California, in a house overlooking a beach, teaching rather than practising journalism and living a lifestyle which sounds pretty comfortable, if her breakfasts are anything to go by:

She'd got up with Sophie and they'd eaten breakfast on the deck together – peaches, bananas, grapes and walnuts chopped up and sprinkled with Grape Nuts, freshly squeezed orange and grapefruit and, for Lindsay only, the industrial-strength coffee she still needed to kick start her day (*Booked for Murder*, p7).

However, even with the new lifestyle class is not a forgotten issue, although, in the context of the 1990s, it is represented in personal rather than political terms:

The service flat in St John's Wood was a reminder to Lindsay that Meredith and Penny inhabited a different financial dimension from her and Sophie. While Meredith was making coffee, Lindsay prowled the room, noting the deep pile of the carpet and the expensive brocade of upholstery and curtains. The weekly rate was probably double the monthly mortgage on the house in Half Moon Bay (*Booked for Murder*, p28).

Given this emphasis on class, Val McDermid's point about 'not preaching' could be read as not promoting feminism as was hinted at an earlier point in the interview: 'We've done being serious and sitting around having our consciousness raised; it's nice to be able to relax within your own culture' (Brooks, p13).

'Relaxing within our own culture' is probably for many lesbian feminists, including myself, a major attraction of the Lindsay Gordon novels, on one level at least. Lesbian fiction remains sufficiently rare for it to still be a joy to read stories about worlds we know or can relate to and which address issues of relevance to us. However, on another level, I wonder whether 'our culture' was or is sufficiently secure for relaxing in. While the media insists that it is 'cool' or 'chic' to be lesbian in the 1990s, the reality is that anti-lesbian violence and discrimination did not disappear with the arrival of equal opportunities policies. Lesbians continue to be threatened in their jobs and as mothers.[5] Further, as Val McDermid addresses at many points in the stories, there are also tensions within feminist and lesbian networks, making them challenging and sometimes uncomfortable, as well as relaxing spaces. The example of class and inequality in lesbian relationships is one tension. Another stems from feminist awareness that the personal is political and its implications for our choices and compromises in relation to work. This surfaces in the reader's first introduction to Lindsay Gordon. We find her sitting on a train, thinking about the contradictions between her feminism and her chosen occupation, a theme that resurfaces throughout the first three of these mysteries:

> In the unreal world of popular journalism which she inhabited, she was continually faced with tasks that made her blood boil. But like other tabloid journalists who laid claim to a set of principles, she argued that, since popular newspapers were mass culture, if people with brains and compassion opted out the press would only sink further into the gutter. But in spite of having this missionary zeal to keep her warm, Lindsay often felt the chill wind of her friends' disapproval. And she had to admit to herself that saying all this always made her feel a pompous hypocrite (*Report for Murder*, pp3–4).

In the early 1980s, the feminist tenet 'the personal is political' put the subject of authenticity higher on feminist agendas than it is in the 1990s, when many former feminists are retreating into lifestylism, and the charge of political correctness is used to discredit those living according to principles other than self-interest. During the late 1970s and early 1980s, it was a sufficiently powerful politic to lead many feminists into either struggling with the split personalities essential for dealing with contradictions or giving up on paid employment and following principles, but in relative poverty. Many of the demands of the world of straight work, including Barbie doll dress codes, were anathema to feminists of the period. Lindsay Gordon resolved the immediate difficulty of traversing the social worlds of tabloid journalism and the peace camp by carrying a crease-resistant change of image in the boot of her car:

Lindsay emerged from the public toilets...a different woman. Before they left the camp she had retrieved her emergency overnight working bag from the boot of her car, and she was now wearing a smart brown dress and jacket, chosen for their ability not to crease, coupled with brown stilettos that would have caused major earth tremors at the peace camp (*Common Murder*, p49).

But the issue of authenticity goes beyond clothes. For many women in middle-class jobs like teaching, social work and journalism, feminist analysis leads to the realisation of the ways these roles belong to patriarchal control structures. They require the promotion of the dominant values which feminism seriously questions. Perhaps, then, it is unsurprising that Lindsay ultimately rejects journalism, though in having her settle for teaching journalism, Val McDermid illustrates that it is rarely possible for a feminist to fully escape the contradictions of living and working in a patriarchal world.

Val McDermid's reference to 'our own culture' makes assumptions regarding the audience or readership of lesbian detective fiction, as it is clear that the Lindsay Gordon books were written for us. The interview with Libby Brooks opens with McDermid identifying 'angry women' as her audience: 'I think that's one of the reasons why a lot of women both write and read crime fiction – it's a place to put our anger' (Brooks, p12). She goes on to say, 'We all want a bit of fantasy, and a reassurance too that it is possible to be a strong woman and achieve the solutions in our lives that we aspire towards – and have fun' (Brooks, pp12–13).

The attributes offered here are positive ones, though whether the 'We' reflects the full diversity of lesbian and feminist communities is a question to be considered. Inclusion is defined through the readers' subjectivity and position in relation to major power structures, gender, race, age, class and relation to heterosexuality as a social institution. As a white lesbian, I feel included by the narrative; they are stories of white lesbians and lesbian networks, predominantly. The few black lesbians present are depicted as more vulnerable, reflecting a part, but only a part, of reality for black lesbians. The characters in the stories are at that nice age, between twenty-five and thirty-five, adolescent angst behind them but ageing not yet cause for serious concern. For me inclusion here has to be in memory – memory of energetic earlier years. Images of older women are lacking. Lindsay, aged twenty-eight in the first story, is no Miss Marple and, unlike Stoner McTavish has no Aunt Hermione[6] to consult when the going gets tough. There is only one positive image of an older woman, Pamela Overton in *Report for Murder*, who is described as 'an imposing woman in her late fifties and magnificent headmistress... One of the old school... Very efficient and very good at achieving what she sets out to do. High-powered but human. Talk to her – it's always rewarding if unnerving... She always knows more about your area of competence than you do yourself. But you'll enjoy her... (pp12–13).

Not only are the protagonists of these stories predominantly white, youngish and energetic, they are also, despite being subjected to violence and sometimes accident-prone, for the most part agile and fighting fit. To be fair, though, Lindsay has lost a lover to cancer, and in every book someone meets an untimely and violent death or long-term injury requiring support from the sisterhood. However, the subject of disability or being differently abled in a disabling world is not an issue in these stories.

Moving into the Mainstream

In keeping with more traditional women's crime writing – Agatha Christie, Ngaio Marsh, Margery Allingham and Dorothy L. Sayers, for example – Val McDermid makes an opportunity to explore relationships between women using the convention of context to define a closed circle of suspects. The county-set house party is transformed to a peace camp, trade union conference or girls' school. As well as limiting suspects, and introducing the overlapping worlds which allow for subplots, this technique facilitates an exploration of issues of concern to contemporary lesbians and feminists. In the earlier books these discussions focus on lesbian relationships, heterosexism, sexual violence, peace politics, political process, feminist activism and kitchen gossip. The later books reflect the shift to lifestylism, lesbian mothering and co-parenting which has characterised the lesbian community more recently.

However, it has to be accepted that writing for a lesbian or feminist audience is inevitably writing for a small readership and realistically means being published by a specialist press as upfront feminist writing continues to be far too challenging to produce bestsellers. To make full-time crime writing an economically viable choice, Val McDermid shifted further towards the classic tradition of women's crime writing in creating a heterosexual heroine, Kate Brannigan.

The Kate Brannigan books provide insight into contemporary problems of inner-city crime, drugs, child sex abuse and the exploitation of women in prostitution, adding a radical edge to her more mainstream novels. However, as their popularity illustrates, they share the wider appeal of this genre. In time no doubt Kate Brannigan will join Miss Marple as a nation's bank holiday favourite. Libby Brooks records that Val McDermid 'feels that the success of these later books vindicated her compromise and has had the positive knock on effect of encouraging her readers to read the four earlier Lindsay Gordon novels' (Brooks, p13).

So Who is Kate Brannigan?

Kate is irredeemably heterosexual but, as each story emphasises, she does not opt for a conventional cohabiting relationship with Richard the wimp:

> 'Treat me like an idiot. I'm used to it after all. That's all you think I am anyway, isn't it? Richard the wimp, Richard the pillock, Richard the doormat, Richard who lets Kate do his thinking for him, Richard the limp dick

who can't be trusted to do the simplest of jobs without ending up in the nick,' he ranted (*Clean Break*, p169).

However, given that some women persist in choosing heterosexuality, Kate's domestic life seems to be an ideal model for heterosexual living:

Richard was my lover next door, a funny gentle divorcé with a five year old son in London. I'd at least been able to hang on to enough of my common sense not to let him move in with me. By chance the bungalow next to mine had come on the market, and I'd explained to Richard that that was as close as he was going to get to living with me, so he snapped it up (*Dead Beat*, pp15–16).

Presumably keeping a male lover next door is slightly less oppressive than sharing a house with one. Even then, as Kate Brannigan explains, a woman still needs to assert herself to hold on to some control in a heterosexual relationship: 'At least I've managed to impress on him that there are house rules in any relationship. To break the rules knowingly once is forgivable. Twice means me changing the locks at three in the morning and Richard finding his favourite records thrown out of my living-room window on to the lawn once I've made sure it's raining' (*Dead Beat*, p16).

The ups and downs of lover-boy Richard and his role in helping and hindering Kate's investigations are some of the several humorous subthemes running through the stories. In presenting a heterosexual relationship from a lesbian standpoint, Val McDermid provides a nice reversal of the more familiar phenomenon of lesbians and lesbian relationships being portrayed by heterosexual writers. In contrast to stereotyped and sometimes macabre images of lesbians by straight writers, this representation of men and masculinity provides an additional source of amusement for the lesbian feminist reader. It introduces an element of lesbian subversion into the more mainstream series, raising the question of whether Val McDermid is entering or indeed subverting the mainstream genre.

In addressing this question, I explore the portrayal of lesbians in the Kate Brannigan series. Unusually for a heterosexual woman, Kate Brannigan has as her best friend Alexis, a lesbian and crime reporter, who lives with her girlfriend, Chris the architect. Alex is first introduced in *Dead Beat*: '...we'd hit it off, and over the years she'd become the kind of friend I could go shopping with' (p174).

Alex and Chris remain background characters in *Dead Beat*, but reappear in *Kick Back* in a more prominent role. There, as middle-class professional women with a dream of an ideal home, they become victims of a self-build land deal scam. With Kate Brannigan coming to the rescue, it all works out well. In *Crack Down*, favours are called in and Alex and Chris find themselves assisting in the investigation and providing childcare as Kate Brannigan has to crack a drugs-trafficking ring to free wrongfully arrested Richard the wimp. *Blue Genes* finds Alex and Chris, living in their dream home, looking forward to lesbian motherhood. Kate Brannigan meets other lesbians as she rushes around the North solving unusual crimes. In *Dead Beat* we're introduced to lesbian social worker Maggie, who becomes prime suspect when her lover, Moira, a black lesbian, songwriter and survivor of drugs abuse and prostitution, is murdered. Hired by a male pop star, Kate Brannigan found Moira living free from drugs and prostitution with Maggie. However, instead of celebrating Moira's survival and newly found lesbian identity, Kate delivers her back to the star, who is her former partner and a fundamentalist Christian with reactionary views on women. Rather than exploring the fatal consequences of returning this young black lesbian to the forces of patriarchy, the story focuses on Maggie, depicted as a pathetic controlling woman threatened by Moira's new life and failing to appreciate the demands of male creativity. If such negative stereotypes are the price of bringing lesbians into the mainstream, then it is perhaps time to question this practice.

However, in *Dead Beat* Val McDermid does not invite

readers into the intimacies and intricacies of local lesbian communities, as she does in the Lindsay Gordon novels. Instead, she maintains a respectful distance and takes the opportunity to educate heterosexual readers about lesbian life and death. For example, she has Maggie explaining that homophobia does not necessarily end at death, hence the need for lesbians to make wills: '...a friend of mine was killed in a car crash and she hadn't left a will. The house was in her name, and her family kicked her lover out on the street the day before the funeral. Gay couples don't have any rights. We have to make our own. That's why we made the wills' (p114).

Val McDermid also depicts Maggie as adopting a cautiousness in conversations with heterosexual women. In my experience this is something many lesbians do to protect ourselves from the voyeuristic gaze: '"Let's get one thing straight, Kate," she observed. "I am not going to discuss my feelings with you. I have friends for that. I'll tell you anything I can about what happened... but our feelings for each other and the way I feel right now is nothing to do with you"' (p112).

I read this as part of an educative process in which lesbians are teaching heterosexual women about respect for boundaries. Another example of boundary maintenance can be seen later in the same conversation, when Maggie explains to Kate (and the readership) how heterosexism, here the writing out of lesbian existence, can take a particularly acute form during the grieving process:

'Believe me, the worst is yet to come. And I'm not talking about the police.' Maggie's face had frozen into a cold mask. 'There's no framework for grief when you're gay.'

'I'm sorry,' I said inadequately.

'Spare me the bleeding heart liberal shit,' Maggie flashed back, suddenly angry. 'Just leave me alone' (p118).

Maggie's grief is not infinite. Readers meet up with her again briefly in *Blue Genes*, where we find her in a new relationship.

The question of how Val McDermid represents lesbian experience and existence to an intended heterosexual readership seems complicated, but is central to the politics and practice of mainstreaming. On the one hand, she fails to challenge stereotypes in relation to both sexuality and race in the construction of Moira and Maggie. On the other, she uses social worker Maggie to educate heterosexual readers about the pain caused by heterosexism, while emphasising the need to respect boundaries. Her fifth Kate Brannigan novel, *Blue Genes*, is the most interesting in light of this question. It opens with Alexis telling Kate that her girlfriend Chris is pregnant, and the story of this pregnancy becomes central when their gynaecologist is murdered. This storyline educates the reader about some of the complexities of lesbian motherhood, beginning with Kate's musings on donor insemination:

First they've got to decide whether they want an anonymous donor, in which case their baby could end up having the same father as half the children of lesbians in the Greater Manchester area, with all the potential horrors that lines up for the future.

But if they decide to go for a donor they know, they've got to be careful that everyone agrees in advance what his relationship to the child is going to be. Then they've got to wait while he has two AIDs tests with a gap of at least six months in between. Finally they have got to juggle things so that sperm and womb are in the same place at the optimum moment ... (p32).

However, it soon becomes clear that what is unfolding is not a straightforward donor insemination storyline. Rather we are dealing with lesbian science fiction. Alexis explains to Kate:

'Given that more men are having problems with their sperm production than ever before, the pressure was really on for doctors to find a way of helping inadequate sperm to make babies. A couple of years ago, they came up with this really thin needle that could be inserted right to the very nucleus of an egg so they could deliver a single sperm right to the place it would count.'

I [Kate] nodded, light dawning. 'And somebody somewhere figured if they could do it with a sperm they could do it with another egg...

...And the baby Chris is carrying belongs to both of you?' I [Kate] asked (p62–3).

I suspect that at the moment the fertilising of an egg with an egg, enabling two women to produce their own biological child, is science fiction, but no doubt in time, and with political will, it could become possible. Given that controversy continues to surround lesbian motherhood and specifically lesbian access to assisted pregnancy technology,[7] the appropriateness of what is turned into a lesbian horror story by the malice of the lesbian gynaecologist surely has to be questioned. I am not saying it is not a gripping story or one that cannot be told, but that I would be more comfortable if it was written for an intended lesbian readership, as part of the Lindsay Gordon series. Granted, the harm may be mediated through the introduction of some, relatively speaking, everyday lesbian mothers, as Kate Brannigan spins across Lancashire and Yorkshire pursuing her inquiries. These women and children make for some very positive images. But the storyline becomes a complete lesbian nightmare. While I recognise that, as lesbians, we are as diverse as any other group of women and bad apple theories apply, the evil of the lesbian at the centre of this story puts her beyond recognition. Representations of lesbians as monsters of evil in what is intended to be mainstream crime writing do little to challenge heterosexism.

My argument is not, then, that negative images of lesbians are by definition problematic, but that context matters. Within criminology, for example, the male agenda has become somewhat obsessed with the 'wdits' ('women do it too syndrome') and of course when women do it, it is deemed much worse and far more serious. Not only is there a concern to demonstrate, against a mass of reliable contrary evidence, that women are more violent, more criminal and more dangerous than men, there is an increasing investment in the recycling of 1970s myths of violence into postmodern format. These myths are being reinvoked to claim that men are as victimised as women by domestic violence, rape and sexual assault; 'date rape' is a feminist conspiracy; and if women do get hurt, it's their own fault. They impact heavily on the many women victimised by sexual violence and the relatively few who find themselves up against the law, women for whom there are no Kate Brannigans or Lindsay Gordons to right the wrongs of the criminal (in)justice system.

In mainstream literature, where a lesbian identity is a stigmatised identity, it comes as little surprise to find lesbians represented as monsters or coming to an unpleasant end, as Moira does in *Dead Beat*. However, I was surprised that Val McDermid should choose storylines with so much in common with the homophobic malestream genre. This is not the first Val McDermid novel with a lesbian as the villain of the piece. In *Final Edition*, a convention of thriller writing is broken when Lindsay Gordon discovers the identity of the murderer. While the surprising twist at the end of the tale is dislocating, the construction of lesbian as killer is mediated in several ways. This story was written for a lesbian audience and published by a relatively small press, so is unlikely to impact much on the mainstream understanding of lesbians. In this context, where most of the characters are lesbians anyway, the inclusion of the odd villain is less damning and may be necessary to stop readers becoming bored by variations on the theme of lesbian detective rescuing wrongfully accused lesbian.

However, in her enthusiasm for mainstreaming, Val McDermid has expressed the hope that her new readership will enjoy the Lindsay Gordon series: 'What I'm saying now is that people who read Kate Brannigan are going back to the Lindsay Gordon books and that's great because it's bringing lesbianism into the mainstream and people will hopefully see it as part of the normal spectrum of life' (Brooks, p13).

Mainstream readers may well not care that their shero is a dyke, but it matters enormously to the lesbian feminist reader. Writing for the mainstream has its problems, as I have suggested, but mainstreaming lesbian literature adds another dimension to the issue. In the Lindsay Gordon novels, Val McDermid offers lesbian feminists the 'chance to relax within our own culture', 'a place to put our anger', a bit of fantasy, magic and fun, as well as challenges. However, a book is what it is because of its readers as well as the text. What makes for attractions for lesbian feminist readers could be read and used differently by others. Meaning is contingent on a shared commitment to lesbian feminist ethics, politics and community. I am troubled that by sharing our lives, issues and concerns with others we are giving them knowledge which can become power – over us. Inviting a voyeuristic gaze into lesbian life at a time when anti-lesbianism and heterosexism are as alive and menacing as they ever were is, I suggest, not without its dangers.

REFERENCES

Novels
McDermid, Val, *Report for Murder*, The Women's Press, London, 1987
—, *Common Murder*, The Women's Press, London, 1989
—, *Final Edition*, The Women's Press, London, 1991
—, *Dead Beat*, Victor Gollancz, London, 1992
—, *Kick Back*, Victor Gollancz, London, 1993
—, *Union Jack*, The Women's Press, London, 1993
—, *Crack Down*, HarperCollins, London, 1994
—, *Clean Break*, HarperCollins, London, 1995
—, *Booked for Murder*, The Women's Press, London, 1996
—, *Blue Genes*, HarperCollins, London, 1996

Other References

Brooks, Libby, 'A Place to Put Our Anger', interview with Val McDermid, *Harpies and Quines*, 9 (October–November 1993), 12–13

Devas, Magda, 'Dyking the Detectives: A Prowl Through the Lesbian "Whodunnit" Genre', *Trouble and Strife*, 22 (Winter 1991), 27–35

Radford, Jill, 'Immaculate Conceptions', *Trouble and Strife*, 21 (Summer 1991), 8–12

—, 'A Suitable Job for a Lesbian', *Trouble and Strife*, 35 (Summer 1997), 40–44

Semple, Linda, 'Lesbians in Detective Fiction', *Gossip 5: A Journal of Lesbian Feminist Ethics* (undated), 47–52

NOTES

1 Val McDermid's stories contain elements of both the detective fiction and crime novel genres, genres which seem to be closely linked; the former typically focuses on the detection of crime and the latter more on personalities and motivations.

2 Val McDermid has also written *The Mermaids Singing* (1995) and *Wire in the Blood* (1997) but as these do not feature Lindsay Gordon or Kate Brannigan, they are not discussed here.

3 Kiranjit Ahluwalia and Emma Humphreys were both convicted of murder and sentenced to life imprisonment for killing a violent partner while attempting to resist or survive his violence. Their cases were taken up in high-profile campaigns co-ordinated by Southall Black Sisters and Justice for Women. Subsequently their murder convictions were overturned on appeal and the women freed.

4 A recent discussion can be found in Gillian A. Dunne, *Lesbian Lifestyles: Women's Work and the Politics of Sexuality*, Macmillan, London, 1997, reviewed by Jill Radford in *Trouble and Strife*, 35 (Summer 1997), 40–44.

5 See Radford (1997).

6 Stoner McTavish is the fictional lesbian detective in Sarah Dreher's thrillers.

7 See Radford (1991) and tabloid headlines from 1977.

I would like to give particular thanks to Elaine Hutton, both for her support for this, my first venture into the world of literature, and for her very careful editorial suggestions.

BLACKENING MY CHARACTERS: RACE AND CHARACTERISATION IN LESBIAN FICTION

Anita Naoko Pilgrim

In this chapter I am looking at the creation of black characters in some novels and short stories by black[1] and white lesbian writers. Lesbian organisations are generally keen to acknowledge issues of race, as well as of (dis)ability, class and age. I would like to acknowledge the fair minds and the bravery of those white writers who have struggled to represent black characters in their work but, in the spirit of Audre Lorde's 'An Open Letter to Mary Daly' (Lorde, pp119–23), to critique that work, hoping to move forward from it. It isn't easy for white writers to describe black living.[2] I will explore below some theories which might explain why this is so, to enable white writers to move towards a better understanding of how to overcome their difficulties. 'Race' is a complex and contentious topic and in this short space it won't be possible to discuss all the many fine studies in the field, or to solve the problem of why some people are so badly misrepresented and abused. I offer here only a basis for further thinking. Race isn't, I'm afraid, an area with any easy answers.

The points I wish to emphasise in my theoretical argument are:

- race is a fictional categorisation (and this is exposed when writers try to utilise it in fiction);
- race is a hierarchical system of categories which fits into

our faulty and inefficient creation of ourselves and others as social beings;
- philosophical, psychoanalytic and sociological studies of Self and Other are useful in suggesting how and why this process takes place.

'Race' is an entirely fictitious and invented method of categorising humankind.[3] In her fascinating study *Imperial Eyes: Travel Writing and Transculturation*, Mary Louise Pratt looks at how this classificatory system arose. She identifies the publication of Carl Linné's (Linnaeus') *Systema Natura* in 1735 as a crucial point in time. *Systema Natura* showed that the chaos of the natural world could be *scientifically* ordered. It arranged plants and animals into sets and subsets: species and genera.[4] To the discomfort of many (including the Pope) Linné turned his classificatory eye on humans and put them among the animals (previous systems of classification were along the lines of God, angels, men, animals). By 1758, six subgroups of the species *Homo sapiens* had been developed, including:

American – Copper coloured, choleric, erect. Hair black, straight, thick; nostrils wide; face harsh; beard scanty, obstinate, content, free. Paints himself with fine red lines. Regulated by customs.

European – Fair, sanguine, brawny; hair yellow, brown, flowing; eyes blue; gentle, acute, inventive. Covered with close vestments. Governed by laws.

Asiatic – Sooty, melancholy, rigid. Hair black; eyes dark; severe, haughty, covetous. Covered with loose garments. Governed by opinions.

African – Black, phlegmatic, relaxed. Hair black, frizzled; skin silky; nose flat, lips tumid; crafty, indolent, negligent. Anoints himself with grease. Governed by caprice

(adapted from quote in Pratt, p32).

We are still using this supposedly scientific categorisation of people.

Given that race is a fictional and invented categorisation of people, it begins to become clear why writers of fiction have trouble fitting it neatly into their work. Society functions as if the physical attributes around which we identify – what Stuart Hall has called 'the floating signifier of race' – are what distinguishes black from white rather than a complex of cultural and socio-economic factors. When we come to write down physical attributes as descriptions of a character we are inventing, we rapidly come up against their real uselessness as indicators to distinguish one person from another. To properly situate a character in the reader's mind, an account of pearly skin, blue eyes and straight brown hair gives little to go on. Race is only useful in that it may indicate something of the character's social and political position in the story. It is only too tempting, however, to describe a character as black and allow the reader to assume this means she is also working class.

Why would we want to invent a hierarchical categorisation of human beings into supposed racial types? One argument put forward is economic. Categorising 'Negroes' as inferior humans allowed the exploitation of African peoples in slavery. Against this has to be set the fact that before and during the widespread enslavement of African peoples by Europeans, Europeans exploited other Europeans: working class, convicted criminals and Irish people, for example, in the colonies. It is also true that slavery was not invented by capitalist European society but was practised in ancient Greece and Rome and even some African societies. Pratt's study shows that the classification of humankind arose as part of a huge scientific project supported by commercial interests but not dictated by them. I would argue that this ready-to-hand classification was simply used by commercial interests to justify one of many exploitations, rather than developed for the purpose.

Like race, sex and gender[5] form a hierarchical system. However, it's dangerous to directly compare race and sex/gender. The oppression experienced by black (men) can't be equated in any simple way with that of (white) women. One obvious flaw in such an equation is that it artificially splits the experience of black women into sexism or racism, when as a lived experience the two are most hideously intertwined. Nevertheless, there are certain points of such clear similarity, places where the lines of power seem to be running parallel, if you like, that I think it likely to be profitable to examine the two together. One such parallel is the way in which small physical differences, such as skin colour, hair type and breast size, are invested with symbolic significance and used not just to categorise human beings but to do so in a hierarchy. I would argue that it isn't possible to live in society as we know it without adopting the sexed power positions male and female. I suggest this is also the case with raced power positions. This isn't to say it is impossible to achieve an egalitarian (post-feminist!) world, but to recognise how difficult and frightening such a project may be. We can't imagine how the world might operate without the power structures currently holding us together as a social entity, of which race is one. For this reason, it is extremely difficult for any of us – even those in deprived, powerless positions – to simply let it all go.

One area in which useful thinking on hierarchical categorisation has been done is the philosophical and psychoanalytical examination of Self-hood and Other-ing and the ways in which we constitute ourSelves by defining what is Other than us. Frantz Fanon, for example, was a Martiniquan psychologist whose works have remained classic examinations of racism and colonialism. His *Peau noir, masques blancs* is an essential resource for writers who are dealing with race and characterisation. Fanon regarded racism as an illness for black and white people together: 'I am speaking here, on the one hand, of alienated (duped) blacks, and, on the other, of no less alienated (duped and duping) whites' (Fanon [1986], p29)[6]

One philosopher who significantly influenced Fanon was Hegel. Drawing on Hegel's philosophy, the African-American writer W. E. B. Du Bois developed the concept of double consciousness: a black person has an awareness of the white hegemony which s/he experiences at the same time as awareness of black subordination and suffering. Richard Wright (another African-American writer) referred to this as black people's 'dreadful objectivity'. Borrowing the phrase 'frog's perspective' from Nietzsche, he wrote about 'a situation in which for moral or social reasons, a person or group feels that there is another person or group above it. Yet physically they all live on the same general, material plane' (Gilroy, p161).

These writers all suggest that there is a certain perspective, looking up from below, through which a subordinated group or person may actually have a greater understanding of the whole situation. The subordinated person must understand her/himself, just as the dominant must understand her/himself but the subordinate must also understand the rules along which the dominant operate, because s/he may actually be killed, if s/he doesn't behave accordingly.[7]

This isn't to say that members of the dominant group (white writers) *cannot* understand the workings of subordinated groups (black people); only that you must put in the hard work now, consciously, rather than when you were small enough to be socially trained.

So far I have been concerned to lay out a theoretical background to the study of race, and the ways in which social persons (including black and white lesbian writers) may be constituting Self and Other. I will now look at novels and short stories by black and white lesbian writers, suggesting some more or less successful ways in which writers have tackled creating black characters. I will look at the black character as token, as political being and as allegorical figure, and at the work of Barbara Burford and Anna Wilson as particularly effective examples of characterisation. (I would just like to add that I enjoy the work of Fiona Cooper, Tash Fairbanks, Vivien Kelly, Anna Livia and Anna Wilson. I wouldn't call any of them racist, although I will criticise the ways in which they are working to be anti-racist in a positive and constructive spirit.)

In examining the black character in lesbian prose fiction, the role of the character, her or his function within the story, is a good place to start. Is s/he in the story as an integrated person or to serve some extra purpose such as background colour or token representation?

Anna Livia's short story 'Angel Alice', for example, immediately introduces us to Gaylord: ' "I'll be the only Cape-coloured queer there," said Gaylord' (Livia, p125). This is one way of getting across the potentially shocking fact of a character's blackness for a reader trained to assume white unless proven otherwise: utilising the shock as part of the style of the piece. Gaylord is a witty, intelligent character and conveys information about South African politics. He is not a token, but rather is well integrated as part of the story, by which I mean it would be a different story if he were not there or were white. However, he is not in the story purely on his own terms. He provides the background colour, or the foil, to the blonde and blue-eyed Angel. When Gaylord talks about going for electric shock treatment to try and straighten himself out, for example, the main purpose of telling this story isn't about Gaylord's experience, or the absurdity of trying to use pain to persuade gay men to find women sexually attractive. This is a mechanism for introducing Angel's terror that if she admits her own lesbian desires, she will be given shock treatment. Black people's function in the story, personified in the character Gaylord, is to produce the subject/Self we identify with when we read the story: the white Angel. Angel could not be quite so blonde, so blue-eyed, so Alice-ish, if Gaylord were a white Cape queer.

To move on to tokens, black characters are often included out of a laudable attempt to provide positive role models and fair representation. However many brownie points I'd like to award for effort, on its own this isn't good enough as, if this is the case, the character will be secondary and not integral to the plot. A prime example are the couple Eugenie Lafayette the jazz singer, and Blind Ellen Eternity, her pianist and lover, in Fiona Cooper's

Rotary Spokes. Popping up out of nowhere as the entertainment in the club where Rotary Spokes accidentally picks up a drag queen thinking she is a biological woman, Eugenie and Ellen manage to e-ops[8] Cooper into telling their life story. To be fair to Cooper, they are historically accurate figures, as many African-American women jazz singers were lesbian or bisexual. Also, a key element of Cooper's style involves diverging off after the life histories of minor characters, and Eugenie gets some of the most glittering garments in the Cooper fantasy wardrobe. Nevertheless, these two are as token as the two disabled women in another Cooper novel, *Skyhook in the Midnight Sun.* They have been inserted just to represent black women and however well meaning and well done, this is patronising.

Vivien Kelly attempts to escape tokenising by giving us two black women in *Dirty Work* instead of just one, as most writers do. She works hard to flesh out her characters. For example, she explains how Liz (who is the boss of the central character, Jo) is tough because her work environment is racist. Liz has a trace of a Yorkshire accent; Fred, Jo's flat-mate, is upper class rather than a stereotypical working-class black lesbian. Complex issues such as the racism operating against Liz in her career and Fred's family's snobbery about her working-class white girlfriend are explored. It is of course possible that a mixed heritage Jamaican/Filipina such as Fred might be upper class, but it's more likely that such a person would be African/English because of the patterns of immigration to Britain from the West Indies and African nations. These kinds of detailed filling in of a black character sometimes read to me as if the author is creating a character by copying a real person she has met, perhaps changing a few apparently inessential facts. The gulf between describing anOther person and drawing on your knowledge of humanity to write a character from within itSelf separates white writers from successful depiction of black characters. Describing the skin from the outside means you fail to get under it.

BLACKENING MY CHARACTERS | 113

Although carefully described, Liz and Fred are background characters who could have been tippexed out without any loss to the main story. I am also uneasy about the way that the physique of each is described as sexually attractive with a forthright enthusiasm not even accorded to Jo's lover. Compare the following descriptions (the third extract refers to Jo's lover):

> I took my coffee from him and sat opposite Liz, Our Beloved leader. Black and beautiful, her hair was corn-rowed and beaded, her clothes understated power-dressing: shaped top, smart skirt, flat lace-up shoes. I had fantasies about the body underneath, slim but muscular, skin like melted treacle, tasting smooth and sweet (p6).

> Fred was always dieting, forever eating, and forever thin. Her father was Jamaican, her mother Filipina, a devastating combination. Her grace and beauty turned heads in the street. She didn't talk much about her heritage, maybe because the rest of our household was white. She was no street-sussed sister though (p21).

> She was funny and loving and I waited for the backswing I had learned to expect. Six months later I was still waiting...

> She smiled, but her eyes still showed her concern – they went from grey to blue according to how she was feeling, and at that moment they shone like cornflowers in a summer meadow (p12).

There is an emotional richness in the description of the white lover which is absent from the plain physical attractions of the two black women. The description of Jo's lover doesn't tell us if she is beautiful to anyone else other than Jo, but makes clear that she is lovely as a human being.

In her novel *Fearful Symmetry*, Tash Fairbanks describes an Asian character as sexually attractive: her voice is 'warm, comfortable, with a slight Asian accent...

The same easy, affable voice that made Sam feel an immediate intimacy with its owner...The voice gave an attractive chuckle' (pp85–6). However, Dr Sunita Shilpa is the central love-interest for the (woman) detective, Sam Carter, and at the end of the novel agrees to go on a date with Sam. Proper characterisation isn't about never describing black women in sexual terms but knowing when it is appropriate to do so.

The characterisation of Dr Shilpa does have its problems. We first meet her like this: 'Dr Shilpa's long thin hands fluttered over the desk in front of her, as they always did in moments of stress or anxiety' (p55). Sunita Shilpa's Asian-ness is signified by her name, her 'slight Asian accent' on the phone and constant references to thin, fluttering hands 'like the wings of butterflies' (p55), which 'traced strange peregrinations in the air' (p58). Fairbanks seems to feel a need to pin Sunita firmly down into her racial character with physical attributes: the slight Asian accent in a voice that can make strong, witty and perfectly idiomatic conversation in a televised discussion (pp106–14), the thin, fluttering hands. (Brown of course, but Fairbanks daren't say so, substituting fluttering instead perhaps. This is an understandable impulse, but compare Sunita Shilpa's fluttering hands to the helpless hand of Dorothy in Burford's 'The Pinstripe Summer' – see below. Fairbanks' description tries to evade crude race characterisation, but Burford's adjective 'helpless' is necessary to the story and isn't standing in for anything else.) While Fairbanks employs the stereotype of the gentle little Asian woman doctor, she also subverts it by making Sunita Shilpa the head of an abortion clinic. My argument is with the need Fairbanks feels to anchor an otherwise well-depicted and integrated character in physical attributes of race. It would be so easy to drop these and let Dr Shilpa emerge as a strong, sensible, sensitive, beleaguered (Asian) professional (woman) without her having irritating ethnic habits.

Token representation is not effective in my opinion because it is based on some notion of an essential difference between black and white. The black must be visibly, definitely different to merit a special corner of our own, to be inserted into the text in a token way. Rarely (if ever), therefore, does an Asian character get to represent the Other-ness of race without being backed up by someone a bit more authentically dark (Fairbanks' *Fearful Symmetry* is an exception). The failure of token representation to fully satisfy and the artificiality of colouring in a few background figures to make things look better expose the wholly artificial nature of race in society. Yet black people exist and struggle with racism.

In her fables, Suniti Namjoshi removes colour as an indicator of race, or exaggerates it to absurdity. She uses satiric humour to expose the absurdity of human behaviour. We can't assign a race identity to the Blue Donkey. Namjoshi represents difference as animals, exaggerating our situations in allegory. In *Pelican*, for example, the pelican is far stronger than, and the natural predator of, the fish. When the fish cries out, 'there are fish among us ... who are willing to see pelicans as fellow fish', we realise the absurdity of the subordinated inviting the dominant to be one with them. The Blue Donkey, who has told this fable, asks her disciples if the pelican was evil and if the fish was a fool. They get into an immediate muddle and give a series of wrong answers. But neither the Blue Donkey nor Namjoshi herself gives us any 'right' answers. They leave us all (reader/disciples hoping to learn from the fable) floundering at the end:

'Are you pelicans or are you fish?'
'Both?' said the disciples anxiously, hoping that at last they'd got it right (Namjoshi, p217).

There is no single simple, right answer to the predatory problem of 'race', which is a daily lived experience for those who must walk about with the near-hallucinatory powers of Du Bois' 'double vision'. Namjoshi shows us the disciples (ourselves, black and white), trying terribly hard but getting nowhere because they think too hard about the

Blue Donkey's questions instead of feeling their way through them.

The cow in *The Conversations of Cow* operates in a number of ways, one of which is to make us sympathise – feel with her and with the central character, Suniti. As the story progresses she shows up some stupid assumptions and rudenesses about black people. The story opens with Suniti describing what she perceives to be a vision: 'I'm down on my knees, waiting for the goddess to manifest herself. When I open my eyes, The Cow of a Thousand Wishes is standing before me on green turf' (Namjoshi, p13). Eavesdropping on the cow (a.k.a. Bhadravati/B./Baddy) and some friends later in the story, Suniti hears the following exchange:

'Where on earth did you find her?' 'Her' – they must mean me.

'In a park in Toronto. She was kneeling on the grass. She looked so peculiar that I walked up to her. When she opened her eyes, we got into conversation.' Well, I suppose they do mean me.

B. giggles. 'She thought I was a goddess' (p71).

The belief that Asian or African women are more holy or spiritual beings because of our race can be quite as uncomfortable and irritating as the belief that we are stupider or sexier than white women.

Because the central character with whom we identify in *The Conversations of Cow* and who is making racist blunders is black herself, the depictions of these behaviours don't come across like a lecture on white racism. In addition, Namjoshi can explore sensitive issues such as the fact that black people may also make racist errors:

'When did you come to Canada?' I ask.

'Oh, a few years ago. How did you know I was an immigrant cow?'

How not to be personal? Or rather, how to be personal

and politic as well.

'I'm from India myself.' I wonder if this constitutes a *non sequitur*.

'Oh,' says the cow. It evidently does (p14).

The issues become more complex in the hilarious account of the cow passing. To start with, Suniti messes up in a restaurant:

'Everything all right, sir?'

'Yes, thank you, but I am not a "Sir", I am a lesbian, and my friend is a cow.'

'GET THAT COW OUT OF HERE.'

...

'Oh,' says Cowslip. 'You said who you were. You must learn how to pass' (p23).

After a quarrel about some tins of corned beef, Suniti tracks down Bhadravati in another restaurant. Because she is a white Brahmini cow, she is passing as 'a large white man chomping away at the edge of a pizza' (p25): 'She sets off down the street with an appalling swagger, jostles everyone, one or two people are knocked off the pavement. I follow in her wake. At the street lights Daddy crosses on a flashing green. A sports car comes to a screeching halt. The driver is a woman. She yells something. Daddy yells back, "You fucking cunt!"' (p26). The combinations of race and sex/gender (later in the story Bhadravati also becomes an Indian woman), the horrendous way in which, for example, white maleness is constituted as an identity and the mechanisms of passing are all exposed by Namjoshi's inventive playing with the categories in animal allegory. Namjoshi's technique might be seen as the furthest extreme from the way in which Cooper and Kelly represent black characters. Physical details such as hair or colour are allegorised into meaninglessness. The political situation of dominant and subordinate, Self and Other, is the hinge on which the fable is hung, the point of the story.

Barbara Burford's 'The Pinstripe Summer', on the other

hand, is not a story hinged around the political situation of race but a delicate and complicated love story about a (black) woman's love for a valley and/or for another (black) woman. It contains possibly the finest representation of a black character in lesbian prose.

I put the word black in brackets. Dorothy's black-ness is integral to 'The Pinstripe Summer', she is the central character, this is her story. More than this, though, Burford operates a total acknowledgement of Dorothy as a black woman. For example, there is a particular character to her love for the green valley she sees from the train because we know, reading the story, that black people are not supposed to feel a sense of belonging to England's green and pleasant land. If black people have any place in Britain, it is in the cities. Although the story is drenched in awareness of Dorothy's black-ness, Burford describes not one physical attribute of Dorothy: skin colour, hair, cheekbones. Even when Dorothy presses a hand against the window of the train carriage in the first few paragraphs, it is not black or brown or cinnamon, nutmeg, coffee, or any other food colour, but helpless.

Of course we assume Dorothy must be black, just because we know Barbara Burford is black, but Burford confirms this for us only by reference to the political: 'although she was tall, assured, and always well groomed, she was not the desired type, colour or age, for a status symbol personal assistant' (p14). This technique is successful because it comes across simply as good writing, not as a technique for the correct representation of character. We don't notice at first that physical race referents aren't there. In my first critical account of 'The Pinstripe Summer', I actually complained because they weren't! Mea culpa.[9]

On the introduction of Willoughby, Burford talks about Dorothy's search for 'people like her' in H. Rider Haggard books. With Willoughby, Burford uses quite different characterisation techniques: the shock tactic (similar to Anna Livia's description of Gaylord), a name that suggests black identity and a cultural referent – Willoughby has beads in her hair. The beads are the main sign, the noise they make reminds Dorothy of Haggard's description of Zulu warriors before Willoughby herself appears: 'Tall and Black and skinny; her skin gleaming as if she oiled it' (p17).

I think the most convincing black character by a white writer I came across was Gloria in Anna Wilson's *Altogether Elsewhere*. Gloria's black-ness is never stated or described, and if Gloria and Tam are token representations, all the other characters are too: lesbian, working class, upper class – Wilson's intended project is to represent a group of differently identified women. Wilson's race characterisation works by suggestion rather than bald statement of skin colour or parental nationality. It's Gloria's name that first suggests she isn't white, and then her smile at the complaining nursery attendant: sunny instead of false, a clever depiction of the way a black woman may use the stereotype of herself as big-smiling, easygoing, to avoid difficult confrontations. Wilson doesn't say Gloria is a big woman but gives us an account of her swaying on the bus: baby and bag 'heaped to her breasts', then a hand searches 'across the flesh of her thigh'. Again the confirmation of her black-ness is in a political act of racism: 'As Miss Hudson remarked, you, Gloria, may play a chocolate drop. I think Louise makes a more suitable sugar plum fairy, don't you' (p12).

I'm still going to nit-pick, and say I'm not convinced by a black household kept like Gloria's. The tinned pineapple and peanut-butter sandwich in the fridge, wearing a crumpled wrap, stealing the iced cakes grandmother has brought round for the family – these sound more to me like a working-class white household. Black people are more prone to represent black households in terms of food from 'back home', which we value and hoard partly as an affirmation of our cultural identity.

I pick this nit because it brings me back to my basic critique of the characterisation of black people. Black people aren't black *because* of a skin colour or nose shape, however much those floating signifiers are attached to certain identities, but because of a political position in the hierarchies of Self and Other. To try to describe a character in terms of dark skin colour is going to fail as surely as anchoring a character in pale skin. Rotary Spokes isn't a white colour, she's big to emphasise that she's a butch motorbike dyke. Jo from *Dirty Work* isn't white and sexy, she's a housing worker. Certainly, it will mean a lot of hard work to properly research the real feel to living life as someone who is characterised black, perhaps as much hard work as living that way.

The importance of creating black characters in fiction is not about political correctness or generously giving black women readers someone with whom to identify. It is necessary to do so because black people are 'really' out here in the 'real' society novelists are writing about. To fail to depict any characters who are different to yourself is to fail as a writer. White lesbian writers need to think about why, if they find they can depict people of other dress sizes, ages, sex and class but not race.

Between 1856 and 1858, the white male heterosexual painter William Powell Frith worked on a painting of Derby Day in which he put a black man – just as one among a very large crowd. He put the man in not for Victorian reasons of political correctness, but because black people were there. I'd like to think that in a century and a half we might have moved on a bit from Frith's approach to representing black characters.

REFERENCES

Novels and Stories

Burford, Barbara, 'The Pinstripe Summer' in, *The Threshing Floor*, Sheba Feminist Press, London, 1986

Cooper, Fiona (1988), *Rotary Spokes*, Serpent's Tail, London, 1995 edn

—, *Skyhook in the Midnight Sun*, Serpent's Tail, London, 1994

Fairbanks, Tash, *Fearful Symmetry*, Onlywomen Press, London, 1996

Kelly, Vivien, *Dirty Work*, Onlywomen Press, London, 1995

Livia, Anna, 'Angel Alice', in Anna Livia and Lilian Mohin, eds, *The Pied Piper: Lesbian Feminist Fiction*, Onlywomen Press, London 1989

Namjoshi, Suniti, *The Conversations of Cow*, The Women's Press, London, 1985

—, 'Pelican', in Anna Livia and Lilian Mohin, eds, *The Pied Piper*, op. cit.

Wilson, Anna, *Altogether Elsewhere*, Onlywomen Press, London, 1985

Other References

Appiah, Anthony, 'The Uncompleted Argument: Du Bois and the Illusion of Race', in Henry Louis Gates Jr, ed, *'Race', Writing and Difference*, University of Chicago Press, Chicago, 1986, pp21–37

Butler, Judith, *Gender Trouble: Feminism and the Subversion of Identity*, Routledge, New York, 1990

—, *Bodies That Matter: On the Discursive Limits of 'Sex'*, Routledge, New York, 1993

Fanon, Frantz (1952), *Peau noire, masques blancs*, Editions du seuil, Paris, 1995 edn

—, *Black Skin, White Masks*, Charles Lam Markman trans., Pluto Press, London, 1986

Gilroy, Paul, *The Black Atlantic: Modernity and Double Consciousness*, Verso, London 1993

Hall, Stuart, '"Race" as a Floating Signifier', the Sage
    Anniversary Lecture, delivered at Goldsmith's
    College, London, 1996
Harding, Sandra, *The Science Question in Feminism*,
    Open University Press, Milton Keynes, 1986
Hegel, *The Phenomenology of the Mind*, trans. J. B.
    Baillie, George Allen & Unwin Ltd, London, 1949
Lorde, Audre (1980, 1984 and 1988), *The Audre Lorde
    Compendium*, Pandora, London, 1996 edn
Oakley, Ann (1972) , *Sex, Gender and Society*, Gower,
    Aldershot, 1985 revised edn
Pratt, Mary Louise, *Imperial Eyes: Travel Writing and
    Transculturation*, Routledge, London, 1992
Solomos, John, *Race and Racism in Britain*, Macmillan,
    London, 1993

NOTES

1 Argument rages about whether the term 'black' (or 'Black')
should be used only for people of African origin (the
American style) or for a broader coalition of ethnic identities
who are not white (original British usage). I find the lack of
clarity about this term useful in that it symbolises the
problematic nature of the whole issue of 'race'. I would be
very concerned if someone came up with clear definitions for
the terms 'black' and 'white' – the sort of hard-line
distinctions used, for example, by Nazis to define 'Jew' and
'Aryan'. I use the term deliberately vaguely as shorthand for
those from 'ethnic minorities'. I don't even know myself who
I mean by 'black' but I hope you will recognise yourselves.
2 It is easier for black writers to describe white characters
but it is harder for us to write at all and to be published if
we do overcome the racism, homophobia and sexism of daily
life and the writing and publishing worlds sufficiently to put
pen to paper.
3 For an opposing argument to this statement see especially
Appiah.
4 Genera is the plural of genus.
5 Ann Oakley was one of the first feminists to begin using
'sex' to mean physical differences between male and female,
and 'gender' for socio-cultural and behavioural differences.
Recently, however, postmodern feminists – in particular
Judith Butler – have argued that there is no such distinction.

6 'Je parle ici, d'une part, de Noirs aliénés (mystifiés), et
d'autre part de Blancs non moins aliénés (mystificateurs et
mystifiés)' (Fanon, 1995, p25).
7 There are obvious similarities between these theories and
what are known as feminist standpoint theories (see
especially Harding), but I don't want to complicate this
chapter by going into the matter here.
8 I have made up this verb from the semi-acronym for equal
opportunities.
9 See 'A Literary Movement', in Valerie Mason-John, ed,
*Talking Black: Lesbians of African and Asian Descent Speak
Out*, Cassell, London, 1995.

I would like to thank Elaine Hutton for asking me to write this
chapter at precisely the moment when I needed a boost in
self-esteem and for being such a supportive editor, and Paul
Gilroy for his invaluable critique and support of my work.
Thank you too to Lilian Mohin at Onlywomen and Helen
Windrath at The Women's Press for digging out books for me.
(None of these people are of course responsible for any
erratic thinking on my part.)

BEYOND SEX AND ROMANCE? LESBIAN RELATIONSHIPS IN CONTEMPORARY FICTION

Lynne Harne

I have been reading lesbian feminist contemporary fiction on and off since the early days of the women's movement in the 1970s. For me as for many other lesbian feminists, such fiction provides not only enjoyment but also at times affirmation of lesbian feminist identity, and on occasion it has reflected and contributed to debates about lesbian feminist politics. With some notable exceptions, however, I have found representations of lesbian feminist personal relationships in such fiction problematic. They are often imitative of heterosexual literature and present images of lesbian intimate relationships that are either highly romanticised or from the libertarian end of the spectrum, pornographic and objectifying of women, with some novels utilising both types of representation. Moreover, representations of friendship between lesbians which are not sexual and other types of important relationships that lesbians may have, such as political and work relationships, are infrequently foregrounded as the subject matter of lesbian novels.

As such we are left with ideological messages about lesbian identity and politics which can be profoundly reactionary. Such messages convey the impression that in order to be a lesbian you have to be in a romantic and sexual relationship and that the fundamental goal of all lesbians is long-term domestic coupledom. Lesbians who are not in such relationships are viewed as 'sad and lonely' or sexually and emotionally 'unfulfilled'. Long-term coupledom is also seen as the only means of providing real security and safety for lesbians. The ideologies of 'falling in love' and/or sexual desire and attraction are viewed as unquestionable and unchallengeable emotions. These may be presented from an essentialist perspective as 'natural' feelings or from poststructuralist and psychoanalytic perspectives as being so deeply embedded within our psyches that they are out of our control.[1] Lesbians who are not in a sexual and emotional relationship are regarded as constantly being on the look-out for such a relationship or recovering from the last one. Perhaps such representations in what purports to be lesbian feminist fiction are not surprising, given the current paucity of political debate and discussion around lesbian personal relationships.

While lesbian feminists have highlighted the institution of heterosexuality as one of the cornerstones of patriarchal control of women, the ideologies of romantic love and of long-term 'monogamy' have been only spasmodically challenged and although issues such as autonomy and inequality have been addressed *within* lover relationships, the powerful discourse of coupledom, and a recognition that this can work against women's autonomy and the sustaining of feminist movements, has not been seriously critiqued in recent years. Julie Bindel and Joan Scanlon (1996) suggest that there has been a retreat into unquestioning coupledom by lesbian feminists as a response to the sexual exploitation and objectification of women represented in the sexual libertarian and S & M debates of the 1980s, and that there is an assumption that 'couple-structured relationships' are the only (moral) alternative to 'SM culture'. This retreat has been increased by material considerations such as fears of economic insecurity as the welfare state has diminished and by the professionalisation of feminist politics whereby the public and private worlds have once again become politically separated. This gap between the public and private has to a large extent been filled by therapy, which has not only depoliticised lesbian personal relationships to such a degree that it is almost impossible not to talk about them in psychological terms[2] but has also had a profoundly negative effect on questioning the benefits of the couple relationship.

Much therapy for lesbians appears to be oriented towards reinforcing couple relationships: examples include couple counselling for relationships that are on the rocks; therapy to spice up your sex life when so called 'lesbian bed death' occurs (perhaps they just found something better to do); therapy for lesbians who love too much (what about the ideology of romance here); and therapy to 'recover' so that you can move on to the next relationship. Perhaps most insidiously the therapist becomes a synthetic substitute friend, a friend who will provide a sympathetic listening ear but who won't challenge you politically about your life.

The assimilationist politics of the lesgay movement, which has dispensed with feminist analysis, has also had an impact. This movement is campaigning for the legal recognition of lesbian and gay marriages and for lesbian and gay couples to have the same social rights as heterosexual couples, rather than challenging the assumptions of dependency involved in such policies and the ideology that it is desirable that everyone should live in couple relationships. The widespread adoption of the term 'partner', which tends to sound like a business arrangement, is an outcome of this type of politics.

On a more positive note, there do appear to be the beginnings of renewed theoretical debate on the politics of lesbians' personal relationships among lesbian feminists, including questioning the practice of prioritising and valuing the sexual couple relationship over and above other kinds of relationships, such as close friendships between women. Janice Raymond's ground-breaking book *A Passion for Friends* (1986) was one of the first to theorise the importance of *discerning* friendship in sustaining and building feminist movement, arguing that it is as much hetero-*relations* as hetero-*sexuality* that sustains hetero-patriarchy.

Going beyond the debates on 'non-monogamy' in the

1970s and early 1980s among lesbian feminists, where the issue was seen mainly in sexual terms, Becky Rosa (1994, pp107–8) defines monogamy as 'the ideology that as adults we should primarily bond with one person, meeting most of our [socially constructed] needs from them (sexual, emotional, physical etc.)'. We might also add to this list political, social and intellectual needs. Bindel and Scanlon stress that the concept of monogamy was developed by men to prescribe sexual fidelity for women, and was not ever meant to apply to men. They argue that it is the enforcing of 'emotional monogamy' through the practice of couplism that is damaging to the development of intimate friendships and to sustaining lesbian feminist political networks.

Rosa also questions whether the very real feelings of insecurity that lesbians experience actually diminish in exclusive couple relationships. While such relationships may for a time provide a sense of safety from a patriarchal heterosexual world, the impossible demands often put on such relationships to make up for all kinds of insecurities invariably fail and result in relationship break-up. Friends are then turned to for emotional and social support, until a new relationship starts and the friend(s) may once again become less important than the new lover. She argues that so much time may be taken up in developing and sustaining a couple relationship that this allows little time for building feminist community and political activism.

Some lesbian feminists do attempt to practise their personal relationships in a different way, but, as Bindel and Scanlon emphasise, this is difficult to do in the current political and cultural vacuum where any questioning of romance and coupledom can appear 'unreasonable or judgemental'. In the early days of second-wave feminism, the ideology of romance was challenged far more than it is today, when any sexual relationship between lesbians is often now referred to uncritically as a 'romantic relationship', to distinguish it from and give it more value than (non-sexual) friendships.

Lesbian feminists have also problematised the male-defined concepts and language of personal relationships as applied to women, arguing that in the twentieth century a false dichotomy between sexual intimacy and friendship has been created, where only the former is supposed to carry with it close feelings of intimacy (Rosa, 1994). But there is also a danger in attempting to turn the clock back and romanticising friendships. Raymond warned against sentimentalising or assuming any natural capacity for women to be friends with each other, as happened in the early days of the movement. It cannot be assumed that we can be friends with all women, or that 'politics and friendship' always go together. Friendship can operate in many different ways and on different levels; nevertheless, many women experience friendships which are important in organising for political change and/or have considerable impact on their lives.

The confines of male-defined language remain. While lesbian feminists have attempted to replace the romantic connotations of the word *love* with others to describe all different kinds of close relationships and friendships between women, such attempts have so far been unsuccessful. Words such as affection[3] seem hopelessly sentimental for the beginning of the twenty-first century, and we are left with inadequate terms to describe the different kinds of personal relationships that lesbian feminists may have with each other but that do not fit into the prescribed categories discussed above.

In looking at the representation of lesbian relationships in contemporary lesbian fiction I have not attempted a comprehensive review. I have revisited a few 'classic' novels which seem to me to go beyond and challenge male-defined ideas of what lesbian relationships should be. Given what I have said above, it will be obvious that I have not looked at the specific genre of lesbian romance fiction! I also look at the representations of lesbian relationships in some recent lesbian fiction within one of the most popular current genres, the lesbian crime thriller.

Before starting, I do have to mention one novel which I have often heard referred to as the ideal model of what a lesbian lover relationship should be: *Patience and Sarah*.

This book, purportedly written as a historical novel about a relationship between two women in the early nineteenth century, was first published in the United States in 1969 and in Britain in 1978. As Bonnie Zimmerman (1992) has pointed out, it encompasses most of the elements of the western heterosexual literary traditions of love and marriage: 'the transcendent mystical and even religious' connotations of true love, where the lovers are isolated from the (real) world and escape into a 'world of their own making' and 'the domestic comedy of marriage' which serves as a 'symbol of harmony, balance and unification' (p78).

In *Patience and Sarah* the two women find a sense of 'coming home' in their relationship when they escape to the 'Greene County' and build their own home and bed, which also symbolically serve to represent a safe haven from a hostile world and a sign of domestic bliss. It is this lethal combination of romantic love and domestic harmony to which some lesbian feminists still seem to aspire, and which continues to be reproduced in a number of subsequent cultural representations.

Ambiguous Romance and Friendship in *The Price of Salt*

It has of course been argued that historically there was a need to produce novels that represented lesbian sexual relationships as being happy and positive as opposed to many of the sad, bad representations of pre-second-wave lesbian literature (Zimmerman, 1992). But by the 1950s there were a few lesbian novels which stood out as questioning the ideal of romantic love and which foregrounded the importance of lesbian friendship. One such novel is *The Price of Salt*.

The Price of Salt was written by Patricia Highsmith using the pseudonym Claire Morgan and was first published in 1952. It was republished by Naiad in 1984 still under the pseudonym of Claire Morgan. In the 1990s Highsmith finally declared herself as the author and it was republished in Britain by the Bloomsbury Press and

Penguin under the less political title of *Carol*. I first read the book in 1984 when it was republished and it had particular resonance for me and other lesbian feminists and lesbian mothers at the time, because one of the major themes of the book deals with a lesbian mother losing custody of her daughter. It is this 'price' of being a lesbian that the original title no doubt refers to.

The book has frequently been mentioned in historical and critical accounts of twentieth-century lesbian literature and has been represented as a novel of romantic love – one of the first to be written where there was a 'happy ending'. But this description does not do justice to the way the novel deals with such themes as the complex tensions between best friends and lovers and the importance of women's friendships. Further, as the novel develops Highsmith shows through her two main characters that she is both ambiguous and sometimes very critical of the ideal of romantic love. Through the plot the naïve and anxious young hero of the story, Therese, is cured of some of her romantic notions and is educated into the 'real facts of life', largely by Carol, the older woman with whom she develops a relationship. Towards the end of the novel Therese discovers what it means to live as a lesbian in a hostile patriarchal world. But there are also some positive possibilities, as she manages to achieve her ambition to be a stage designer and she discovers that there are other lesbians in the New York artistic world in which she moves.

At the beginning of the novel Therese meets Carol when she is working temporarily as a sales assistant in the toy department of a large store. Carol is a rich customer buying a Christmas present for her eight-year-old daughter. Highsmith presents this meeting as a classic instance of 'love at first sight'.

> Their eyes met at the same instant, Therese glancing up from a box she was opening, and the woman just turning her head so she looked directly at Therese...Therese felt sure the woman would come to her. Then Therese

saw her walk slowly towards the counter, heard her heart stumble to catch up with the moment it had let pass, and felt her face grow hot as the woman came nearer and nearer (p31).

The irony of this passage is underlined by a crucial incident at the end of the novel. Therese asks Carol why she came over to her in the store. She replies, 'For such a dull reason. Because you were the only girl not as busy as hell' (p265). Therese at this point can laugh at her own naïve romanticism.

Highsmith also challenges the idea that developing a sexual relationship should mean cutting off from close friends or not maintaining and building friendships with other women. Therese is initially puzzled by Carol's mysterious close friendship with Abby, who is always there, standing out from the background. Before they have become lovers Therese asks Carol who Abby is. Carol replies simply, 'Abby is my best friend' (p73). Therese at first experiences Abby as a threat and rival to her developing relationship with Carol, particularly when Abby engineers a meeting alone with her, to, as it appears, check out her motives for wanting to get to know Carol. Later she discovers that Carol and Abby have also been lovers and at one time set up a furniture shop together, but that their sexual relationship had ended after two months. Therese is confused by Carol's revelations that she can fall in and out of love with someone so quickly and sees Carol as being cynical about love. Towards the end Therese has accepted Abby's close friendship with Carol. It is Abby who has kept a watch on Carol's interests while she has been away on a trip with Therese and who informs Carol that her husband had engaged a private detective to follow them. It is also Abby who remains in contact with Therese and sends her money so that she can return to New York and talk to Carol, who had to return alone to fight for custody of her daughter.

Therese also learns from Carol the importance of valuing women's friendships in other ways. There is a curious incident at the beginning of the book when Therese makes friends with a fifty-year-old woman who works at the department store. Therese is initially repelled by Mrs Robicheck's age, her physical disabilities and ugliness. But then when the woman asks her to come and talk to her sometimes in the store, 'the woman's ugliness disappeared, because her reddish brown eyes behind the glasses were gentle and interested in her. Therese could feel her heart beating, as if it had come to life' (p7).

A few days later she approaches Mrs Robicheck outside the store and is invited to eat with her. Therese accepts and Mrs Robicheck offers her a dress she has made when she had her own dress shop. While Therese is trying on the dress, she again becomes repelled by Mrs Robicheck, who becomes in her imagination 'the hunchback keeper of the dungeon'. Therese waits until Mrs Robicheck falls asleep and then 'escapes'. The significance of this apparently incongruous episode does not become apparent till much later when, on a month's trip with Carol, Therese thinks about sending a present to Mrs Robicheck, but she hesitates. Carol tells her to send the present, as if stressing the importance of maintaining the friendship with the older woman. Later in the novel when Carol has broken with Therese, in order to be allowed to maintain contact with her daughter, Therese in her less naïve state independently keeps up her friendship with Mrs Robicheck by writing to her.

Therese wants to spend all her time alone with Carol on their trip, but Carol befriends a widowed woman who is taking a holiday of her own. Mrs French was 'about seventy, with a Maryland accent and a hearing aid, ready to get out the car and climb anywhere, though she had to be helped every foot of the way' (p203). When Therese questions why they have to go everywhere with Mrs French, Carol asks her, 'Did you ever think you might be seventy-one, too, some day?' (p205).

Throughout the development of their relationship, Carol attempts to warn Therese against idealising lesbian relationships in a patriarchal world that regards women as male possessions. She describes the way her husband, Harge, had picked her out 'like a rug for his living room' (p125). Later, after she and Therese have become lovers, she tells Therese how he tried to control her and resented her having any independent life of her own. In conversation with Therese she states:

> 'You know that, don't you ... in the eyes of the world it [lesbianism] is an abomination.'
> The way she said it Therese could not quite smile. 'You don't believe that.'
> 'People like Harge's family [do].'
> 'They're not the whole world.'
> 'They are enough. And you have to live in the world' (p189).

It is following this episode that they discover that Harge has engaged a private detective to follow them and that Carol's custody of her daughter is threatened. Thus Highsmith emphasises that a lesbian relationship cannot be a romantic escape from the world.

It is Carol's breaking off her relationship with Therese, in order to be allowed to maintain contact with her child, that finally disillusions Therese of her own beliefs that love means you invest all of yourself in the lover relationship. Therese initially experiences Carol's actions as betrayal, yet she very quickly recovers and sets about furthering her career as a stage designer.

While the novel ends in an anticlimax when she and Carol do finally agree to live with each other (the happy ending so often quoted and which appears at odds with the rest of the plot), both characters have gained more autonomy in the process. Carol has had to give up any aspirations to have access to her daughter, because she wouldn't agree to stop being a lesbian, but has taken a job and has not been destroyed by her custody battle, and Therese has realised that she shouldn't sacrifice her career for the sake of a lover relationship.

'Which one of us is going to kill the other first?':
Non-monogamy and Community in *Sister Gin*

Sister Gin (1975) by June Arnold stands out as a novel
emerging from the American lesbian feminist movement
of the 1970s which presents a direct critique of the ideal of
the long-term, sexually monogamous lesbian relationship.
The main narrative of the novel deals both humorously
and at times very painfully with the disintegration of the
twenty-year-old domestic relationship of two middle-aged
white women, Su and Bettina.

The novel opens with Bettina, an alcoholic, still in bed
in the late afternoon, waiting for Su to come home from
work. In these opening pages Arnold brilliantly satirises
the notion of a safe haven from the world that is
represented in the ideal domestic relationship of *Patience
and Sarah*. In bed (the symbol of domestic harmony and
bliss), Bettina fantasises about her love for Su, their
lovemaking and the security that their relationship
represents.

It was five when she woke up smiling. Su would be
home soon, would hold her more, would tell her what
her raw mind had to know – that the day was fine, that
they two were safe now from work, from money, from
traffic and jostles of the street; that they two needed
only a couch and a tiny space to rock each other in (p4).

Bettina literally shuts out the world by keeping it
always dark: 'Other people did not expect dusk at five
o'clock in August North Carolina. In Bettina's room it was
always as dusk as she could make it. But not empty: Su's
smell of herbal handlotion and brazen aftersex pricked her
nostrils.' There is a problem though. Bettina finds she
cannot summon the effort to get out of bed, and the safe
haven becomes almost like a prison. There is also the
constant fear of Su leaving her: 'Suppose she [Su] doesn't
come back?' When Su returns, Bettina's worst fears are
realised. We learn that Su is acknowledging to herself that
she doesn't love Bettina any more and they quarrel. Su

asks, 'Which one of us is going to kill the other first?' (p10).

Their quarrel is interrupted by a visit from Mamie Carter, an independent seventy-seven-year-old woman who is an ex-actress and a contemporary of Bettina's mother. During this visit Mamie Carter introduces her theory that 'people don't drink enough', that if enough gin is drunk it can liberate the brain into creativity.

'Sister Gin' becomes Su's *alter ego*. It is through her that Arnold introduces a device whereby Su begins to question her own beliefs about relationships. Sister Gin makes her question the value of Bettina's nurturance in their relationship through stating:

> You are smothered by Bettina and her mothering, her breast which works in reverse to suck back juices from your mouth. Her reassurances leave you filled with rage, to vent into soft air.
> The best women do not see beyond their daily pleasures; what makes them feel good is no more than what has always set women up – flattery, prettiness and smiles, attention (p69).

After she commences a sexual 'affair' with Mamie Carter, she also debates the meaning of monogamy between women:

> S. G.: Monogamy is the old-fashioned arrangement whereby one partner profits at the expense of the other. It means only possession.
> It means to be possessed by love.
> And assurance that the offspring of the fickle woman is also the offspring of the named, will-writing male (p145).

In reply to this, Su argues that when you are old the meaning of monogamy between women in a relationship changes, because there is no long term as old women die. Bettina also has her moments of self-realisation. She becomes aware that she has seen Su's love as something that would make her strong, rather than the opposite.

But their relationship does not immediately end. Their roles almost reverse when Su loses her job as a book reviewer on the town's conservative daily newspaper for writing a radical feminist critique of a new bestseller. Su also becomes an alcoholic as she struggles to find herself as a radical writer. Bettina becomes the strong one, who takes a job as a television reviewer on the same newspaper and whose work becomes her security. It is Bettina who then ceases to love Su, as she sees her job threatened by Su's disintegrating lifestyle and her radical feminist activism against pornography and rape.

By the end of the book, Su and Bettina's domestic relationship is over. Bettina's insecurities have been transferred to fears about losing her job. Su has overcome her own fears and insecurities through entering a politically active community of woman-identified women. She calls on all women to enter this community, to 'come in free'.

In this novel Arnold has exploded the myth of the lesbian couple as protective and life-sustaining; rather she portrays it as 'debilitating', working against women's autonomy and preventing women from 'opening out into the world of politics and communal activity' (Zimmerman, p93). She poses the possibility of open-ended relationships operating in a politically active woman-identified community that will free all women. But it is also on this level that the novel fails to some extent to work because the women's community which is portrayed is fantastical, and, as Arnold recognises in her Epilogue, also profoundly racist, since it excludes and fails to give a voice to black women.

Sister Gin has been represented as ground-breaking in that it challenges ageist stereotypes and portrays both the menopause and old age as positive and liberating for women.[5] But the politically active community of women in the book, which is set in a conservative medium-sized town in the Deep South, is not only old, *it is also white and extremely rich*. Some of the women also have black servants. It is these old rich women who have formed a subversive action group against the rapes that are taking place in the town.

While there are some hilarious scenes where the women, in between playing bridge, capture the perpetrators of rape, strip them naked and tie them to boards to be put on display in public areas of the town, there is also a sense of unreality about their actions. It is hard to imagine that, since they have so much invested in the status quo, they would actually take such risks.

Arnold is also careful to make all the rape perpetrators white, and one of the rape victims black (in fact, she is the daughter of one of the women's servants), but the views of the black women involved are not heard in the main body of the novel, and nor are the black women given an opportunity for political activism. Arnold belatedly recognises this lack of subjectivity accorded to the black women in an Epilogue which she devotes to May, Bettina's mother's black servant:

'Miss Su, you haven't forgotten *May*. Oh, I know I'm in there moving around the table, going through the door, but I'm not there. Now you know how you were feeling when those books put you in them. They let you move around a little while and then go on out the door. You didn't *say* anything but pretty soon you got you a Sister Gin to say it for you' (p206).

But Arnold's solution is ultimately to evade giving black women a voice, because she feels she cannot authentically represent them; instead she leaves it up to black women themselves.

In the end her vision of feminist community remains as romanticised as the ideal of the romantic couple relationship which she demolishes, because there is little recognition of the different power positions between women. It was to take black feminism to stress that any sense of political community and friendship between women was something that had to be worked at and could not just be assumed.

'I was supposed to be your friend': Friendship, Power and Conflict in *The Threshing Floor*

The community of women in Barbara Burford's novella *The Threshing Floor* (1986) is far from idealised. Rather Burford stresses that in order for women to be able to work together on common projects, conflicts brought about by personal friendships and differences of inequality have to be recognised and addressed. Through setting the main part of her narrative in a women's glass blowers' co-operative in Kent, she brilliantly illustrates the resentments common to a number of women's collectives, where inequalities created by racism, differences in income and expertise fail to be recognised. Her idea of community between women is one that is both fragile and precarious, and where a sense of unity can be attained only through the hard work of acknowledging and trying to resolve power differences and working through conflicts.

Through her main character, Hannah, she also explores the complex resentments and jealousies that exist from friends when lover relationships are given priority over and above friendships and work relationships.

When Hannah returns to work in the glass-blowing co-operative after she has cut herself off for weeks to recover from her grief at the death of her long-term white lover, Jenny, she discovers that she has to deal with the hostilities that have been created by her own isolationist stance. There is the hostility from a young white woman, Nikki, who herself has felt attracted to Hannah, but whose resentment is fuelled by the fact that, as she is poor, she doesn't have the same decision-making power of some of the other women, who have put their own money into the co-operative. She had also depended on Hannah to get a lift into work. Since Hannah has been away she has had to get the bus from the outlying village where she lives and has been accused of stealing petty cash by other members of the co-operative to help pay for her fares.

There is also the resentment from Hannah's black heterosexual friend at work, Caro, who had expected Hannah to turn to her for support:

'I wasn't offering [to have a sexual relationship with you],' Caro said angrily. 'I was just saying that if you had needed someone to hang on to, to just hold you ... I was supposed to be your friend, and I would have been there for you.'

'You're very good at making people feel that they are important to you, but you're also too bloody good at ignoring them when something else comes up. You're so damned single-minded Hannah, and so downright mean-spirited, you wouldn't even share your grief with us, with *me*!' (p136).

Caro also expresses her resentment at Hannah's lack of solidarity in leaving her 'to cope alone with this bunch of white women' at the co-op and how the white women had resented their closeness.

After a stormy collective meeting of all the workers, Caro raises another conflict between herself and Hannah. When Hannah expresses herself as being on Caro's side, Caro responds:

'My side! How can you be on my side? Because we're the same colour? Let me tell you something, Hannah. You don't live in the real world. *I'm* the only one on my side. When a woman is on her own with a child, she doesn't have time for well-wishers and the right politics. You don't have any idea, you really don't!' She pointed at the bedroom door, 'That's reality in there! And politics and right-onness doesn't matter a damn, when she has to be fed and clothed, and looked after, while you have your endless meetings. And, that's something *you'll* never understand' (p170).

There are also the conflicts raised between Caro and Hannah, when Hannah starts to develop a lover relationship with Caro's friend Marah. When Hannah wants to spend a day alone with Marah, instead of with Caro and her daughter, Zhora, as she had arranged, it is Marah who says they can't let Caro and Zhora down.

All this is the down-to-earth stuff of real-life attempts to deal with the conflicts involved in women's work relationships and the conflicts over priorities raised by friends and lovers. But while Burford recognises the importance of building women's community and the need to give time and attention to friends, it is still romantic love which wins out. In the character of Hannah it is the ideal of committed romantic love which alone can provide a place to be one's own true self, and, as with *Patience and Sarah* there is a suggestion of coming home: 'Love; a thin, fragile, but amazingly tensile thread between them, that allowed one or other of them to find her way back from exile, often self-imposed, to their core' (p192).

The novella ends with Hannah starting a new romantic relationship with Marah in which 'love, passion and compassion all had their place' (p210).

'You give me a lot, you know': Cynical Monogamy in *The Fires of Bride*

By the mid-1980s there was also a more cynical anti-romance stance towards lesbian relationships adopted by some lesbian feminists. While sexual non-monogamy had been rejected as sexually exploitative and manipulative of other women, a more materialist serial 'monogamy' developed, without the need to put the emphasis on 'true love', or to think that it was even desirable that relationships should be long-lasting.

This stance is reflected in Ellen Galford's wonderful parody of Gothic romance, *The Fires of Bride* (1986). In this novel the hero, Maria, a London-based out-of-work artist, accepts the offer of the mysterious and sinister Catriona to stay at her castle on the little-known Hebridean island of Cailleach. Being penniless, Maria accepts the 'hospitality' of Catriona and becomes her live-in lover. Catriona sees herself as Maria's patron and hopes that in return for her 'hospitality' Maria will once again be inspired to paint, but predictably the power imbalances in their relationship work against Maria's inspiration, and she spends most of her time in bed, while Catriona works as the island's only doctor.

When, after six months, Maria thinks about leaving because she feels 'half-way between a kept woman and a parasite', Catriona ironically lists a number of good practical reasons why she should stay:

> 'You give me a lot, you know. You're here, you keep me from feeling lonely, you're someone to talk to in the evenings, but you don't get in my way. And you feed the cats when I'm off the island. And now you've finally learned to cook a bit, you're practically indispensable.'
>
> 'And is that all I'm good for?' [Maria asks.]
>
> 'What more do you want?' snaps Catriona (p197).

Maria finally decides to leave the castle a few weeks later, when it appears that Catriona is starting a sexual relationship with the only other dyke who occasionally lives on the island, Stoney, an ambitious archaeologist. She recovers her sense of autonomy and artistic inspiration after a mysterious visit from her *alter ego*, the seaweed woman, and when she is no longer materially dependent on Catriona.

Later in the novel she has a more 'open' sexual relationship with Stoney where there are no commitments made on either side. For Maria a sexual relationship has become less important than her work and her 'political' involvement with the women of the island as a whole, helping to sustain the island's economy and defeat the patriarchy, symbolised in the character of the minister of the kirk.

In Galford's representations of relationships there are echoes of *Sister Gin*. The domestic live-in relationship is depicted as one that can induce weakness and dependence. Autonomy is obtained through creative and feminist work and through a wider sense of community. Any sexual or domestic relationship, while it can be enjoyable and bring other benefits, is not the most important means of sustaining lesbian identity or existence.

But Galford is also critical of sexually 'non-monogamous' relationships. For the power-hungry Stoney, her own lack of commitment appears as a means of scoring over other women. When she tells Maria she is returning to Edinburgh because her archaeological season is over, she resents the fact that Maria is not upset at her leaving. Maria challenges her:

'Do you want me to get out my widow's weeds? Throw myself in the wake of your departing ferry? Come now.'

'I guess I'm used to people being a little more – upset when I go.'

'You don't look too upset yourself.'

'Ah but I'm the one doing the leaving. You're the one left behind on this godforsaken island' (p164).

Moreover, when Stoney describes Maria's relationship with Catriona as one that depicts Catriona as a vampire, 'living off the blood of younger women', Maria defends the relationship, stating that her time with Catriona was a period of germination, when she gave her something she needed (p163).

Through Stoney's and Catriona's spite and jealousy towards each other, which they both express to Maria, Galford also demonstrates the real conflicts that are created around sexual relationships and the nastiness that this can cause. Maria tries to take a more ethical position by refusing to disparage either of them, but the illusion that lesbian feminists are automatically nice to each other is gone for ever.

The 1990s and the Lesbian Thriller

By the end of the 1980s the inevitability of the lesbian couple relationship and/or the sexual objectification of women by women were dominant and recurring representations, particularly in what has become perhaps the most popular genre of lesbian fiction, the crime thriller. Although lesbian thrillers do have a specific appeal to lesbian feminists (see Radford and Hutton, this volume), in their representations of lesbian relationships they often reflect the worst aspects of misogynist backlash culture or a retreat into sentimental coupledom.

Sarah Dreher's Stoner McTavish novels are the most obvious examples of the latter. While the Stoner novels often provide a good read in terms of their plots, it is the characterisation that I find so problematic. Stoner is represented as a neurotic and emotionally insecure butch investigator who needs constant nurturing reassurance from her sidekick and lover, the feminine Gwen. As Judith Beckett has suggested, Gwen has little personality and she acts more like a traditional wife than an equal in Stoner's investigations. In the first novel (*Stoner McTavish*, 1985), Stoner has heroically rescued Gwen from a murderous husband and subsequently it appears that Gwen has to be eternally grateful by dedicating her life to boosting Stoner's fragile ego (and patching her up when she is physically injured by villains). In each novel Gwen and Stoner declare their undying love for each other, Gwen calling Stoner 'honey' and 'dearest' in true femme fashion. (Incidentally Gwen wears a night shirt and Stoner pyjamas, just to underline their butch and femme roles! [*Bad Company*, p155])

Stoner also has a kind of parody of a feminist support group, in her heterosexual friend and business partner Marylou, Marylou's mother the psychiatrist, Edith Kesselbaum, and Stoner's mystic aunt, Hermione. Oddly, in all the Stoner novels I have read, she seems to have no close lesbian friends, except the occasional lesbian couples she meets in the course of her investigations. A lesbian friend would no doubt be too sexually threatening in Stoner's cosy little set-up, where lesbianism is always perceived as being limited to the sexual only.

Contrasting with the sentimental romanticism of the Dreher novels are the 'tough investigator' novels of Mary Wings. But these go to the opposite extreme and often glorify sexually violent and objectifying representations of relations between women. Her early novels, such as *She Came Too Late* (1986), celebrate sado-masochistic feelings and practices and the objectification of women.[6] In her later novels such representations are normalised. In *She Came by the Book* (1995) Emma Victor, the gritty thirty-something detective, is sexually titillated by the appearance of the youthful Fresca.

> I found myself looking at the tender juncture where her jeans struggled to cover the paisley boxer shorts of silk. The silk stretched, almost shiny, like a patterned sealskin over her pubis.
> 'Any closer and your face is going to be in her lap,' Rose whispered but she was watching her too, watching the way her clothes moved over rippling ribs' (p45).

In *She Came to the Castro* (1997) gay male pornographic representations are presented as something to be celebrated as examples of sexual freedom, and those who oppose them, such as the female villain character, are portrayed as fascists. At the end of the novel Emma goes home to celebrate being 'just another voyeur' and watches a pornographic video of the two lesbians around which the plot centres.

These representations often take place alongside traditional romantic and domestic ideals, since the hero, Emma, combines her objectification of women with wanting a romantic and long-term domestic relationship, thus depicting the final assimilation of lesbians into mainstream patriarchal culture.

In *She Came by the Book*, Emma has set up house with her lover, Frances, in a middle-class neighbourhood of San Francisco, and Frances has reinvented herself as 'A lipstick lesbian' (p9). In this novel there is a complete slippage into heterosexual language to describe Emma and Frances's relationship. When Emma is about to have a sexual 'encounter' with Fresca, she states, 'The apartment of my marriage floated away from us' and 'Adultery was just as I remembered it. It was wonderful' (p74) and, in the sequel to this novel *She Came to the Castro*, the end of her relationship with Frances is described as a divorce. Ironically, in the latter novel the gay community is campaigning against the Marriage Act, which will outlaw lesbian and gay marriages. Both these later novels are also located in and around gay male settings. In *She Came by the Book*, the setting is the Lesbian and Gay Archive, which was 'a huge marble edifice', which the 'Lesbian Revengers' had pointed out was in its style, 'overtly and completely male ... indeed it was hard not to see massive erect penises in the phalanx of pillars' (p20). In *She Came to the Castro* the central action is set in the middle of a showing of a gay men's pornographic film at a gay film festival, where a giant phallus is flashing across the screen.

While Wings may be parodying the complete assimilation of male gay and heteropatriarchal values by the lesbians in her books, such parody remains ineffectual because she offers no feminist alternatives to the world she is presenting. There is, for example, no debate on why lesbians might want to get married in the first place in the discussion Emma has with her neighbour on the need to oppose the Marriage Act. Emma merely argues that it needs to be opposed because it is yet another example of the state's homophobia.

In *She Came by the Book*, Wings does satirise therapism, the obsession of dealing with lover relationships in a confessional way, through the character of Deborah Dunton, a lesbian therapist and author of the best-selling *Lesbians Who Love Too Much*. In the following incident, Emma requires some assistance from Deborah in the solving of the murder. The therapist is being uncooperative.

Then she started to shake her head. I'd have to try some magic words.

'The relationship is going really shitty with Frances,' I confided. It was just the aperitif for Deborah's appetite.

'It isn't!' Then, 'I'm so sorry.'

'Really. It's just as you said Deborah. I think Frances is tired of my intimacy issues.'

... It was working. Deborah switched on her therapist gaze and knitted her eyebrows in a familiar way...

'Emma have you read my book?' (p148).

But Wings does not question the inevitability of the lesbian domestic relationship when Emma and Frances break up; the assumption at the end of the book is that Emma will move on to yet another one.

The lesbian thriller is supposed to be 'escapist literature', but escape from what? The reader can no doubt enjoy representations of lesbians triumphing over 'evil' men and sometimes 'evil' women, but in their representations of lesbian relationships many of these books in the 1990s present boringly repetitious ideological messages that differ very little from heterosexual popular literature.

Of course there are exceptions. The Ellen Hart detective novels make for a refreshing change, with the sidekick and confidante of the investigator a close friend rather than a lover. But in these novels, endless descriptions of food seem to act as a kind of sensual substitute for the absence of romance and sex in the relationship between the friends Jane and Cordelia, and when one or other of the friends has a lover these relationships are also compared to food. In A Small Sacrifice (1994), Cordelia describes her 'romantic' relationship with Mugs as being 'better than chocolate truffles from the St Paul Hotel' (p24). Romance can even triumph over food it seems!

Some recently published thrillers do offer a more complex analysis of lesbian relationships and represent the importance of friendships and lesbian networks in sustaining lesbian feminist resistance to heteropatriarchal values.

Silent Words (1996), a recent US lesbian feminist thriller by Joan M. Drury, questions the ideology that only a lover relationship is special. Tyler, the hero and investigator of the story, in searching out her near relatives to find out the truth about her mother's background, asks her cousin Sonny, who has a large household of children, whether she has a special relationship in her life. Sonny replies, 'Lots of special relationships. Most of them under fifteen. And others who are friends not lovers...I get tired of that question sometimes. You know, the only "special" relationships are between lovers...' When the question is turned around on Tyler, she replies that she has 'lots of special relationships, with women who are dear friends and with women I work with' (p30). She also states that she is not sure whether 'love' really exists. Towards the end of the novel, when her best friend starts a lover relationship, she describes her own jealousy at the difference this makes to their close friendship. Feelings of jealousy from close friends as opposed to lovers are infrequently discussed in lesbian novels, as friendships are not supposed to evoke intense emotions.

The lesbian protagonist in Maggie Kelly's *Burning Issues* (1995) conducts her war with the pornography industry against the messy background of a decidedly unromantic on/off relationship with her lover, Sue, the hideous realities of living with a teenage son and the solidarity and criticism from her network of lesbian feminist friends.

In a humorous dig at lesbian romantic ideals the novel opens with the hero, Mig, in bed with her lover, but she can't sleep because of Sue's snores: 'I slept. Sue snored. I woke up. She stopped...Sue snored, as if she'd been waiting for me to drop off. I turned over carefully without sighing. The last time I sighed she jumped awake in a rage at my "moaning"and denied snoring. In the morning she'd apologised, but it was just another nail in the coffin' (p1).

The novel also raises the problems created for friendship networks when lovers fall out, and reflects in a dialogue the unresolved approaches to the way lesbian feminists deal with jealousies and resentments when sexual relationships break up and new ones begin. After Mig and Sue's relationship is apparently over and both of them find themselves at the only lesbian and gay club in town, Mig, who has decided she can't be in the same place as Sue, is challenged by one of her friends.

Gill was exasperated. 'Why do you both have to let it

make such a difference?' She meant couldn't we part without creating a schism in the group? 'You're behaving like a couple of heterosexuals – it's ludicrous!'

'Just because we're women – '

'And feminists, so-called – '

'All right,' I sighed, 'but you're letting ideology get the better of you.'

She looked as if I'd punched her in the nose.

'For God's sake, Gill, this is reality. The problems are the same whatever relationship you're in...'

'They shouldn't be,' she called after me as I walked off... (p63).

Unfortunately, as so often happens in real life there the debate ends, not moving beyond the cynical 'realist' position, that emotions constructed within a heteropatri-archal framework cannot be changed, or the idealist position that women and feminists should act differently from men.

In *Burning Issues* the dilemmas raised by the conflicts and jealousies between ex-lovers and friends are too neatly and idealistically resolved through the plot, with friends and ex-lovers uniting in political action. Mig and Sue once again become lovers as a result of Sue joining in the struggle against the murderous patriarchal villains, and snoring ceases to be a major bone of contention between them.

This novel also raises another important factor that can occur in lesbian sexual relationships: the impact of sexual abuse. When the relationship between Mig and Sue initially ends, Mig begins a brief sexual, 'non-romantic' relationship with a woman in her lesbian friendship network. Kelly describes their initial sexual encounter in the fairly standard trite terms that appear in the majority of lesbian novels which aim to avoid pornographic repre-sentation. But during the second encounter Mig is afflicted by the pornographic images she has seen of her murdered friend and ex-student, Dulcie. In contrast to the Wings novels where Emma Victor's sexual relationships are excited and aroused by pornography, these images invade and violate Mig's own sense of her sexuality and she is unable to continue to have sex.

Burning Issues paves the way for a new type of lesbian feminist political novel that could represent the complexity of trying to change the way we behave in close relationships in connection with feminist politics and resistance. But unless there is less cynicism about the politics of personal relationships and renewed open discussion among lesbian feminists such representations are likely to continue to be few and far between.

REFERENCES

Novels

Arnold, June, *Sister Gin*, Daughters Inc.,Vermont, 1975 edn, The Women's Press, London, 1979

Burford, Barbara, *The Threshing Floor*, Sheba Feminist Publishers, London, 1986

Dreher, Sarah, *Stoner McTavish*, Pandora, London, 1985 edn; The Women's Press, London, 1996

—, *Bad Company*, The Women's Press, London, 1995

Drury, Joan M., *Silent Words*, The Women's Press, London, 1996

Galford, Ellen, *The Fires of Bride*, The Women's Press, London, 1986

Hart, Ellen, *A Small Sacrifice*, The Women's Press, London, 1994

Kelly, Maggie, *Burning Issues*, Onlywomen Press, London, 1995

Miller, Isabel, (1969), *Patience and Sarah*, The Women's Press, London, 1979 edn

Morgan, Claire, (Patricia Highsmith), (1952), *The Price of Salt*, Naiad Press, Florida, 1984 edn

Wings, Mary, *She Came Too Late*, The Women's Press, London, 1986

—, *She Came by the Book*, The Women's Press, London, 1995

—, *She Came to the Castro*, The Women's Press, London, 1997

Other References

Beckett, Judith E., 'How to Meet Lesbians', *The Lesbian Review of Books*, III, 1 (1996), 30

Bindel, Julie and Joan Scanlon, 'Barking Back' *Trouble and Strife*, 33 (Summer 1996), pp68–72

Raymond, Janice, *A Passion for Friends: Toward a Philosophy of Female Affection*, The Women's Press, London, 1986

Rosa, Becky, 'Anti-monogamy: A Radical Challenge to Compulsory Heterosexuality?', in Gabriele Griffin,

Marianne Hester, Shirin Rai and Sasha Roseneil, eds, *Stirring It: Challenges for Feminism*, Taylor and Francis, London, 1994

Zimmerman, Bonnie, *The Safe Sea of Women: Lesbian Fiction 1969–1989*, Onlywomen Press, London, 1992

NOTES

1 The psychoanalytic 'out of control' perspective is reflected in the novels of Sarah Schulman, which I do not propose discussing in this chapter as I do not consider them feminist.

2 See, for example, Celia Kitzinger and Rachel Perkins, *Changing Our Minds: Lesbian Feminism and Psychology*, Onlywomen Press, London, 1993.

3 Raymond (1986) refers to 'gyn/affection', but this is not a term which has ben widely adopted by lesbian feminists.

4 See, for example, Gabriele Griffin, 'History with a Difference: Telling Lesbian Herstories', in Gabriele Griffin, ed, *Outwrite: Lesbianism and Popular Culture*, Pluto Press, London, 1993.

5 Sally Munt in *Murder by the Book? Feminism and the Crime Novel*, Routledge, London, 1994, discusses such representations in a positive light and describes them as harmless!

ZERO TOLERANCE IN WONDERLAND: SOME POLITICAL USES OF IMAGINATION

Elaine Miller

The literature of 'imagined worlds' has obvious attractions for both lesbian writers and readers wanting to protest about the way things are and to explore and promote different ways of being. Released from the constraints of realistic narratives, settings and characters, lesbian writers are free to employ a variety of subversive techniques to create imagined worlds which sharply critique aspects of the real one. These worlds reflect the various ways we are thinking about ourselves. They contain our experience, express our anger, validate our ideals and consistently place us at the centre.

This chapter looks at some of the ways in which lesbian writers of the 1970s and 1980s created fictional worlds of dream and nightmare, to explore imaginatively a variety of contemporary lesbian issues. It locates some representative texts within a tradition of the interlocking genres of utopian, dystopian and science fiction writing by women and speculates on the contribution of these texts to the shaping of feminism today. It questions the cultural power of such fictions: how far can they be seen as agents of social change?

This favourite genre of the previous two decades is significantly sparse in the lesbian fiction of the 1990s. It seems that today's individualist and integrationist ideology has little use for a fictional form that offers such opportunities to challenge whole social systems and imagine autonomous female existence. This is a genre for radical times and its moment will no doubt come again. For the time being, it is interesting to explore it as part of the distinctive spirit of the early years of the modern feminist movement.

The novels and stories referred to in detail are *The Female Man* (1975) by Joanna Russ, *Motherlines* (1978) by Suzy McKee Charnas,[1] *The Wanderground* (1979) by Sally Miller Gearhart, *Daughters of a Coral Dawn* (1984) by Katherine V. Forrest, 'London Fields' in *The Needle on Full* (1985) by Caroline Forbes and *Bulldozer Rising* (1987) by Anna Livia. Reference is also made to *Herland* (1915), Charlotte Perkins Gilman's utopian novel which mapped out much of the territory that is further explored by these later writers.

None of the texts discussed does anything so futile as to offer a blueprint of the definitive lesbian world, so the question of how we get from here to there does not, *in that sense*, arise. Within this approach, qualms about the suggestion that cataclysmic events are necessary before radical change can occur become irrelevant: the holocaust of Charnas' *Motherlines*, the near destruction of the Y chromosome of Forbes' 'London Fields' or the glamorous race through deep space of Forrest's *Daughters of a Coral Dawn*, although thematically significant, are in the main examples of 'displacements', narrative distancing devices common to the genre, to set apart the imagined from the real worlds they are critiquing.

Utopian narratives can be read on different levels and from different angles. Some of them can be read straightforwardly along their narrative lines as creations of dream worlds into which the reader can relax and enjoy the fantastic celebration of an idealised, sometimes hilarious, lesbian world. This offer of temporary escape from the pressures of real life is an important function of this type of writing.

At the same time, there is what Jean Pfaelzar has described as 'the political defiance inherent in utopias' (pp14–15) and the humour of such texts is often used as one of several powerful tools to express this defiance.

Katherine V. Forrest's marvellous Mother in *Daughters of a Coral Dawn*, for example, subverts the ubiquitous stereotype of the older woman, the witch, the magically powerful female who uses her power only to oppress and destroy. Mother is sure that her many daughters will always 'manage' and of course they always do, whether it's a case of rounding the Einsteinian curve to give the pursuing spaceship the slip, or working out how to deal with the evening hurricanes on their new planet. Much earlier, Charlotte Perkins Gilman had used satirical humour brilliantly in her utopia *Herland* to expose, among much else, oppressive essentialist views of female nature and some of the grosser excesses of male conduct.

The Wonderland Tradition

Deborah Rosenfelt has offered a useful thematic description of feminist utopias and their efficacy, suggesting that they work by 'conscripting readers as participants in the same linear evolution', while 'the narrative enacts the central feminist myth in its purest form – a woman's progress from passivity to action, from weakness to strength, from victimisation to oppression, from oppression to liberation' (p273).

All the novels and stories discussed here do this, the 'woman's progress' they chart being explored in the context of women's community and relationships and in opposition to men.

Jane Donawerth and Carol Kolmerten have looked at the literature of imagined worlds 'in the historical context of the development of western feminism'. Tracing a women's utopian tradition from the seventeenth century through to the end of the nineteenth, they see the particular frameworks chosen as well as the issues addressed in these utopias as arising directly from the situations and preoccupations of contemporary feminists. The seventeenth- and eighteenth-century feminist goal of education for women produced imaginary worlds of women learning in women's communities, in seclusion from men, on island paradises, in cloisters, libraries, salons, and large country houses (pp4–7). What was once a dream explored in these fictions is now, happily, a reality. Women's colleges have been one of the generators of feminist movements and girls' schools are now whisking away the best academic prizes (*The Times*, 30 August 1997).

Predictably, though, such communities are again being threatened in the 1990s, not now by men disguised as women deliberately to deceive but by transsexuals making out a political case to be admitted as women.[2] It is no longer possible to be sure that any group described as women-only will be just that: transsexuals are showing up at them more and more nowadays. Even holiday centres advertised as women-only find themselves accommodating transsexuals and there are recent examples of women-only groups actually splitting along different policy lines on the issue of whether to admit male to female transsexuals who want to join.[3]

Nineteenth century utopias reflected changing feminist goals, exploring issues of suffrage, divorce, careers, property rights and introducing scientific ideas (Donawerth and Kolmerten, pp4–7). These socialist and liberal feminist preoccupations clearly inform Charlotte Perkins Gilman's ground-breaking early-twentieth-century utopia *Herland*, with its intense focus on economic, domestic, educational and political reform for women: an imaginative reworking of her non-fiction classic *Women and Economics*. In her novel, Gilman built on and developed earlier traditions such as pastoral settings, the belief in the efficacy of education and women-only communities. In addition, she mounted a very powerful challenge to gender-stereotyping and the oppressive cult of femininity. Her ideas are still ahead of much social practice and remain a challenge, particularly as the current backlash against women has resulted in the return to biologically determinist views, apparently validated by the results of various genetic research projects published in recent years which claim to have found evidence that 'gender roles are determined genetically' (*Guardian*, 9 June 1992) and that 'what we might call feminine intuition...is a set of skills of genetic origin' (*Guardian*, 7 May 1997).

How to produce children without men is a powerful central theme in this area of women's writing. In Gilman's utopia, evolution sees to it that the women develop autonomous reproductive powers. Some of the later novels anticipate current reproductive technology. A recent newspaper report on research carried out on animals, for example, outlined a technique which was full of implications for lesbian feminist separatists and bore uncanny similarities to the ideas in the imagined worlds of lesbian feminist writers, in particular, those of *Motherlines*, 'London Fields' and *Bulldozer Rising*:

> Instead of two sets of chromosomes, one each from the mother and father, they will all come from the mother, creating only female offspring and effectively dispensing with the need for males...although it raises the prospect of an all-female world, experts believe there are ethical and medical objections to extending it to humans because of the dangers of inbreeding...Limited research on non-viable human eggs left over from infertility treatment in Britain has found they will begin dividing spontaneously

This research, as might be expected, was stopped because, 'We did not go any further than division to eight cells because our main interest was to find out more about what a real fertilised embryo was doing' (*Sunday Times*, 16 March 1997). Clearly, the prospect of reproduction without men was too terrifying to face.

Such preoccupations remain central to the lesbian feminist writers of the 1970s and 1980s, although worlds very different from Gilman's utopia are created in response to, for example, the increased experience of community, friendships and relationships which lesbian feminists had, by then, gained; changes in the wider social, scientific, economic and political contexts within which lesbian feminists have to operate in the real world; and the persistence of male sexual violence. Terry is still around (see below).

Zero Tolerance

How to respond to male sexual violence so that it is controlled and finally defeated becomes the major focus for utopian, dystopian and science fiction writing by lesbians during the two decades of the genre's popularity in the 1970s and 1980s, especially in the novels and stories of the 1980s. Together with separatism, it is the most clearly identifiable common concern linking widely different envisionings of dream and nightmare worlds during these decades. This appears to be part of the same consciousness that eventually led to the successful negotiation of a common agenda between diverse groups of women around feminist campaigns to combat male sexual violence and to vindicate women who had been convicted of killing violent men. Such feminist alliances were realised in the 1990s within activist groups like Justice for Women.[4] Imagined worlds are very much about the real world.

Separatism, defined as women's denial of access to men, is symbolised in Gilman's *Herland* by a mountain range thrown up by a massive earthquake two thousand years before the story begins. It completely encircles the country. Only women live there. These women have evolved into Herlanders, unexposed to men and heterosexuality for two thousand years. This notion of women's ability to evolve in isolation from men into beings much more powerful than they were within patriarchy is very prominent in the genre in the twentieth century: Janet in *The Female Man*, the Riding Women in *Motherlines*, the Hill Women in *The Wanderground*, all the goddess-like Daughters in *Daughters of a Coral Dawn* and the Rockwomen in *Bulldozer Rising*. In these imagined worlds, this evolution can be read as a metaphor for the benefits to women of separatism.

This concept is radically different from an essentialist view of female nature and should not be confused with it. These women are women constructed in worlds beyond heterosexuality and beyond patriarchy and so, paradoxically, are not women in the same sense that Monique Wittig's 'lesbians are not women' – that is lesbians who will not conform to the norms of male-constructed femininity (p32).

All of these novels and stories address the threat posed by the male desire for access to women-only communities. Through their imagined worlds they explore, in individual and original ways, the same organic connection that theorist Marilyn Frye pinpointed in 1977 between access and power in general and the centrality of this notion to any analysis of lesbian separatism in particular: 'feminist no-saying is more than a substantial removal (redirection, re-allocation) of goods and services because Access is one of the faces of Power. Female denial of male access to females substantially cuts off a flow of benefits but it has also the form and full portent of assumption of power...'

Frye goes on to clarify that separatism, control of access, is an essential strategy for shifting power balances in favour of women, implying that it is not necessarily an end in itself.

In real life, as in these imagined worlds, some men attempt access by force. Marilyn Frye has described a personal experience of this:

> Only a small minority of men go crazy when an event is advertised to be for women only – just one man tried to crash our woman-only Rape Speak-Out, and only a few hid under the auditorium seats to try to spy on a women-only meeting at a NOW convention in Phila-delphia. But these few are onto something that their less rabid compatriots are missing. The woman-only meeting is a fundamental challenge to the structure of power (Frye in Hoagland and Penelope, p68).

Long before Frye, Gilman had noted this fact of life. By the 1970s and 1980s it was still a very stark fact of life, which might go some way to explaining the increasingly hard line taken against men in these later feminist fictions. Gilman was optimistic: her answer (whose contemporary context is partly the suffragette movement) was the collective action of the Herlanders: '"Now for a rush, boys!" Terry said. "And if we can't break 'em, I'll shoot in the air." Then we found ourselves much in the position of the suffragette trying to get into the houses of Parliament through a triple cordon of London police. The solidarity of those women was something amazing' (p23).

This is part of a very funny incident with the deadly serious purpose of reversing in Gilman's imagined world the power structure in her real contemporary world: a technique which she uses brilliantly and often hilariously in her utopian satire.

It was Gilman who introduced the theme of women's response to men's physical and sexual violence into the genre in the twentieth century. In *Herland*, after the earthquake had completely cut off most of the women, children and a few men from the rest of the world, including most of the men in the country who had been away fighting a war, the few surviving men slaughtered the mothers, the old women and the boy children, hoping to take complete power over the country and the young women and girls whom they had allowed to live. 'But this succession of misfortunes was too much for those infuriated virgins. There were many of them and but few of these would-be masters, so the young women, instead of submitting, rose in sheer desperation and slew their brutal conquerors' (p55).

This is very significant: the demonstration in a utopian novel that the ultimate threat to women is men's violence and the ultimate necessity for women is the control and final defeat of that violence. Women reading *Herland* are offered for the first time in utopian fiction a strong, authentic, vicarious experience of the control and defeat of male sexual violence by women's collective action. Even after all other feminist goals have been achieved, this remains the ultimate threat, as becomes clear much later in the novel. After three of the Herlanders have decided to experiment with marriage (of a very unusual kind) Terry, one of the three men who gain access to Herland, attempts marital rape:

> The women of Herland have no fear of men. Why should they have? They are not timid in any sense. They are not weak; and they all have strong trained athletic bodies. Othello could not have extinguished Alima with a pillow, as if she were a mouse.
>
> Terry put into practice his pet conviction that a woman loves to be mastered and by sheer brute force, in all the pride of his intense masculinity, he tried to master this woman.
>
> It did not work. I got a pretty clear account of it later from Ellador, but what we heard at the time was the noise of a tremendous struggle and Alima calling to Moadine. Moadine was close by and came at once; one or two more strong grave women followed.
>
> Terry dashed about like a madman; he would cheerfully have killed them – he told me that himself – but he couldn't. When he swung a chair over his head one sprang in the air and caught it, two threw themselves bodily upon him and forced him to the floor; it was only the work of a few moments to have him tied hand and foot, and then, in sheer pity for his futile rage, to anaesthetize him.
>
> Alima was in a cold fury. She wanted him killed – actually (p13).

Terry is eventually expelled from Herland. The women creating the imagined worlds in the 1970s and 1980s take a harder line. Such men do actually end up dead.

The Female Man is the most uncompromising of the 1970s novels in its answer to the question: what do we do about male sexual violence? Jael, existing in a time long before Janet was born, claims that Whileaway, the earth ten centuries into the future and Janet's lesbian utopian home planet, is the result not of a mysterious plague that wiped out the men (as her ancestors have told her and Janet believes) but of women like the lesbian hero Jael and their radical activism. This activism involved countering violence with violence. Russ takes a harder line than Gilman. Through Jael, Alima gets her wish. Rather than be raped, Jael kills.

Russ anticipates varieties of female reaction to this act through descriptions of the other three Js, all from different historical times. As they watch, 'Jeannine is calm. Joanna is ashamed of me. Janet is weeping. But how do you expect me [Jael] to stand for this all month? How do you expect me to stand for it all year? Week after week? For twenty years?' Then comes the inevitable question: '"Look, was it necessary?" says one of the J's, addressing to me the serious urgency of woman's request for love, the ages-long effort to heal the wounds of the sick soul, the infinite, caring compassion of the female saint...'

Throughout the novel, Jeannine is taut with the oppression of her conditioned romantic femininity. Joanna is enraged by sexism in her profession. Janet is content on her lesbian Whileaway, not wanting to know what strategy had to be employed to make it happen. Jael is locked into a deadly conflict between Womanland and Manland and saying: this is how you get from here to there. The achievement of *The Female Man* is the conviction it begins to create in the reader that Jael is quite possibly right. At the very least, it ends with the rhetorical question: if not this way, how?

Motherlines opens with an urgent sense that the threat of male access must be contained at all costs. Sheel patrols the borderlands, exhilarated that this task has, for the moment, fallen to her:

Riding the borderlands with light rations and three full quivers of arrows made her feel alive as nothing else did; here on the vulnerable outskirts of the plains she felt most strongly the rich vitality of the land she was guarding. Her senses were wide open to the sharp scent of pine, the grate of a pebble under her horse's hoof, the long sunlit lines of the foothills advancing up the lower reaches of the mountains. If men had crossed from the Holdfast, she would know it (p8).

The major dilemma explored at the end of the novel is again to do with access. Should the Free Fems, who have escaped from the Holdfast, be allowed back to challenge the men in an attempt to win the city for themselves? Will this endanger the separatist community of the Riding Women? There is no consensus on this and the novel reaches the philosophical position that once a movement has started, no one can predict where it will go; certainly, no one political viewpoint can control it as it takes on a life of its own.

The world of *Motherlines* has come about by 'the wasting': the nuclear holocaust resulting from man's misuse of technology. Two options for women are initially explored in the novel through the delineation and scrutiny of two types of community: the Riding Women and the Free Fems. Alldera, the central character, moves between the two communities. She finally opts for the Riding Women rather than the Free Fems, many of whom have absorbed several aspects of male and heterosexual attitudes to power and relationships and some of whom seek escape from the harshness of their real lives through the romances of Daya. These are very different from the imagined worlds being discussed here, which stare the real world in the face. The narrative of *Motherlines*, for example, explores the issue of co-operation over time between different and mutually wary women in order, possibly, to produce some creative collectivity.

The Riding Women are evolved women, different in kind from the Free Fems. They are initially the result of the creative opportunism of a group of women used in the genetic experiments of male scientists before the wasting. Following the experiments, these new women possess the complete genetic material to reproduce without men.

They produce only girl children. All that is needed to set the process in motion is the fluid from a horse's ejaculation. Most of the women therefore mate with a young horse once or twice in a lifetime, to ensure the survival of the Riding Women. It is highly ritualised and highly pragmatic. The same horse is also slaughtered for its meat, hair and skin. The women are always in total control. The Free Fems, who have left the city to escape sexual slavery and violence, are horrified by this practice, but as they cannot reproduce without men, they will otherwise inevitably die out. Charnas is making a powerful statement by presenting this ritual as infinitely preferable to contact with men.

In *The Wanderground*, it is the Planet Herself that secures the boundary between the women's world in the hills and the heterosexual world of powerful men and subservient women in the city. She has created a 'force field', a safe geographical area in which men's power, defined in terms of technology and testosterone, becomes non-operational immediately they or their machinery venture outside the city. In the 'remember rooms' the young Hill Women find out about their history, including incidents of horrific violence towards women in the past but also the moment when the 'magic' first happened: two men were about to rape two women when they became impotent. The strands of fantasy and realism are skilfully woven together in the novel. The fantasy creates a world in which male sexual violence is controlled in perhaps the most effective, because the most humiliating, way since the two men witness each other's impotence. The realism resides in the remembered attacks on women which mirror the real world and in particular the rape of Margaret, which takes place in the present time of the novel and signals a threat to all the Hill Women. Especially moving is Seja's deeply empathetic reaction to Margaret's experience (pp22–6).

At the beginning of the novel, the two communities have evolved along separate lines. The central crisis is generated by an apparent weakening in this power boundary. Information about this is passed on to the Hill Women by the Gentles, who resemble some versions of the 'new men' who have emerged in the wake of the women's liberation movement. Towards the end of the novel, the possibility of some co-operation with these men 'dressed much like the hill women' (p183) is explored. The response is tentative. Betha admits that 'her absolutes began to get fuzzy around the edges when she tried to make them apply to a man like Aaron'. She realises with pleasure that Aaron 'could respond to an enfolding of care...He was not a woman, after all, and there seemed only the thinnest possibility of mindstretch between them...women and men cannot yet, may not ever, love one another without violence...but I would trust him with much that is dear to me' (pp124–5). Both sides agree later that 'only time will tell' (p195).

The novel's final position is powerfully and poetically expressed in the litany of the Hill Women at the end. The women will not attempt to slay the men, who must change or die. The novel makes it clear that it is the men themselves who have to do the thinking and the work to bring about this change. Most crucially, they have to want to change; the Hill Women will not put energy into this. Gearhart's position thus differs from Gilman's in that Gilman's women skilfully raise the awareness of the men they meet. However, in her concession that men might be capable of change, Gearhart's position is nearer to Gilman's than it is to either of her contemporaries Russ and Charnas, both of whom present men as sexual violators and as rapists of Nature, undifferentiated and irredeemable.

Daughters of a Coral Dawn comes to much the same conclusion as Russ and Charnas. Although the mood of the novel is an entertaining mixture of humour, sentimentality and melodrama, it suddenly reveals a hard political edge at the point in the narrative when men gain access to the beautiful lesbian planet, Maternas, and sexually threaten one of the Daughters. Decades after Mother and her glamorous, elitist, goddess-like Daughters have settled there and created, by technological wizardry, an exotic lesbian paradise, a ship finds its way through deep space and lands on the planet. It contains one woman and three men from earth who have come looking for the escaped lesbians. Predictably, the men begin by expecting the woman-only planet to be paradise for them. When the woman pilot, Laurel, points out to Coulter, a male colleague, that the inhabitants of 'paradise' might have different ideas, 'Coulter slapped Hannigan on the back and playfully flexed his own muscles, puffing out his chest... "Come on, Laurel. When women have a choice... I mean when women really have a choice – "'. Coulter attempts to rape Laurel. Like Terry before him, he is finally prevented by the collective action of several women.

The realism with which Forrest describes this incident is impressive in its build-up from Coulter's sexist comments, to declarations of 'love' for Laurel, to attempting to kiss her, to attempted rape, to becoming 'a crouching beast of pure menace' as he threatens the woman who has defended her (pp132–3).

Later on, a second pilot, Hannigan, sexually threatens a young woman of fifteen and again, like Coulter, he is foiled, this time by the athletic young woman herself. However, she is emotionally devastated and is found lying 'curled in a foetal position, hands covering her face' (p190) surrounded by a group of women. The romantic, glamorous atmosphere of this novel, set in its coral, gold and silver world, changes dramatically to one of grisly reality as the women break every bone in both the man's hands. Megan attempts to explain to Hannigan's commander, Ross. '"She is fifteen. And has never seen an earthman. To her, you are strange beasts. And she is unaccustomed to the sexual aggression practised by men of Earth, commander. Our finest psychologist advises me that it will take months to repair the damage that has been done"' (p192).

Ross' defence that the man only 'placed a hand on one of you' is immediately corrected by Megan to 'forced a hand on one of us' (p190). Ross exclaims that they can't be expected to understand such nuances of [your] culture, that the men had been in space for months and that, after all, despite everything [i.e. being lesbians] they were women (pp190–93).

The men are made to leave the planet in a spaceship that Megan knows will implode. She also knows that the men will be aware of what is going to happen an hour before it does. It is a decision she takes to safeguard the planet. Male access has turned out, once again, to be traumatic. Although fully supported in her decision by all the women of Maternas, Megan is devastated by what she has had to do. Despite reassurances from the women closest to her, she cannot help feeling for some time that 'It was not right. It can never be right' (p198). Laurel, her lover, who came in the spaceship with the men from earth also has a powerful emotional reaction to what has happened: 'In the company of several other women of Maternas – my sisters now, but strangers to me – I watched Megan send my shipmates to their deaths; and I wept silent tears for them, for my own pain, and most piercingly for hers' (p199).

Nevertheless, the final position Forrest takes on this is that it was necessary to allow the men to die. Their threat to the women's planet was total. Her delineation of the reactions of the women to the solution chosen and their perception of the acute moral dilemma posed by that solution is an attempt to modify any uneasiness a reader might have about callous murder of men. Like Russ in *The Female Man*, Forrest constructs a complexity around the issue while still concluding that there is no other way for women to be safe and free. Like the men in the imagined worlds of both Russ and Charnas, these men also are undifferentiated and irredeemable.

It is remarkable that two novels which are such worlds apart in style and politics as those of Russ and Forrest should focus with such realism on male sexual violence, expressing so much rage and indicating similar solutions.

Enter the Generation Gap

Geographically much closer to home is Caroline Forbes' short story 'London Fields'. The setting is a variation on the popular pastoral or wild-country setting of so many lesbian imagined worlds. The action takes place in London Fields, which 'had finally become fields after all this time' (p80), the fruit, vegetables and pasture supporting the small local community of lesbians who live in the decaying buildings of the city. A male nemesis in the form of a mutating Y chromosome, caused by industrial production of poisonous gases, has eventually led to the destruction of the male population. Only X chromosomes are being produced and only girl children are being born. The XX combination has begun to divide spontaneously and those women who really want children can have them by desiring them. This idea of reproductive evolution based on mind and body harmony to ensure the survival of women is reminiscent of what happened to the Herlanders. Decades of horrific violence followed as the men looked their own extinction in the face.

Julie, one of the main characters of the middle generation, still has nightmares about it: 'She had learnt to fight, to use a knife, everyone did, there was no room for the squeamish. Only once had she killed a man but the memory still woke her up shaking' (p93).

The crisis of the novel is generated by the appearance of a group of young men, most likely test-tube babies from one of the many laboratories set up years before to try to preserve males. It appears that they have been raised in secret by their scientist 'father', now dead. He has told them to come to London, which they seem to regard as their own special religious shrine. They think of him as a god and are guided by 'notes' he has left which they will not allow anyone but themselves to see. They appear friendly and interested in the women, whom their father has described in his notes. Face to face with them, they are surprised that the women appear smaller and weaker than their father's descriptions have led them to believe. This introduces a chilling note into the narrative.

The democratic community of women around London Fields spans three generations. They agonise long and hard in their meetings over what to do about the problem of the men: should they ignore them and hope they will go away; incorporate them; or wipe them out at the first sign of trouble? The younger generation, who have insisted on being allowed to attend the meetings, want to risk trusting the men in the hope that they will be different from those who have died, having escaped their influence. Perhaps they could educate the men, have a positive influence, redeem them? Perhaps it is possible to create 'new men'?

It is after a particularly long and emotional meeting that Sue, an enigmatic woman of Julie's generation, decides to take unilateral action. She is obviously still coming to terms with the effects of something that has happened to her in her past, something she cannot possibly forget but never speaks about. She goes out and shoots all the men dead as they sit around their camp fire. Forbes, like Russ and Forrest, is concerned to explore the complex emotional reactions of the women to this deed. Like them, she cannot avoid the conclusion that it was a necessary act. The poetically sombre mood in which the story ends infuses it with a mythic quality: ·

Julie and Cathy went over to Sue and gently took the gun out of her arms. She looked up at them with calm, open eyes and smiled. She was singing softly to herself, songs the others had never heard. Her old smile had come back and she let herself be carried back to the house without complaint. The rest of the women stood and sat and walked around the scene for hours, till the fire had died out and only the cold moonlight lit up the contours of the living and the dead. Before they departed, each one had approached the bodies and looked into the faces of the dead men. And each one accepted that, by whatever route, the final emotion that gave them a dreamless sleep that night, was relief (p151).

This is a striking short story. It introduces the issue of the ideological generation gap between young lesbians and older lesbian feminists, prominent in the 1980s, suggesting that the young lesbians' more tolerant attitude to men stems from a lessened awareness of the dangers they pose. The story is a validation of the lesbian feminist separatist perspective of Julie and Sue, rooted in the memory of those very dangers. The subtle, allusive quality of Forbes' portrayal of the new men is likewise very arresting. She achieves a strong sense of the sinister threat that patriarchal Christianity might start all over again, as the new men obey the word of their father, revere his notes and head for the promised land of London. Like the Hill Women of *The Wanderground* who have their 'remember rooms', Julie and Sue know that remembering is vital.

Anna Livia's *Bulldozer Rising* takes the generation gap as its major theme. In a city where speed and youth are worshipped, everyone over forty is expected to commit suicide quietly in one of the city's burn-out parks. The old and the sick are reviled and constantly at risk of murder. There are no mothers, but instead a system of 'womb surrender'. Young women give their wombs up to the 'father-possessors', who use reproductive technology to produce children who belong entirely to them. Child sexual abuse, as well as horrific forms of physical and sexual violence, is institutionalised. Gender polarity is extreme: children of the father-possessors are either nellies (young girls conditioned into ultra-femininity) or zappers (young boys conditioned into machismo). It is not a good time or place to be a middle-aged lesbian separatist. Yet the heroes of the novel are exactly that. Taking up the genre's tradition of town and technology in stark opposition to nature and the countryside, the novel finally locates power within the domain of the Rockwomen. It is there that the power to destroy the city patriarchs resides. Like the women of *Herland*, *The Wanderground*, the grasslands of *Motherlines* and Maternas, the Rockwomen are evolved women. Free to progress apart from men, they have developed impressive powers. They live well beyond a hundred years. They have healing powers. They know about a special kind of moss that kills the Y chromosome. The city women take it back, use it and at the end of the novel are making their way to the refugee camp until the

Y chromosome is eliminated and their moment comes.

However, it has been touch and go. The main danger arises when a youngwoman is invited to a secret all-female meeting in what turns out to be a well-meant but misguided attempt by a group of older women to spread the word among the younger generation. The youngwoman, as the wise old dyke Karlin foresees, does tell her youngman but, thanks to Karlin, disaster is averted. This novel, in common with the others discussed, is concerned with safeguarding access and controlling and finally defeating male sexual violence. Like *The Wanderground* and 'London Fields', it highlights the importance of memory and the passing on of remembered experience to the next generation of women. It also contains an impressively powerful analysis of the dynamics of ageism.

Imagined Worlds: Agents of Social Change?

The imagined worlds created by lesbian and lesbian feminist writers of the 1970s and 1980s are novels of protest. They express a commonality of female experience with regard to male sexual violence and its persistence. Not only do they explore feminist theories, they also generate powerful emotional effects. They give a sense of women's collective anger, together with a collective resolve to counter this violence, based always on the realisation that we ourselves are the ones who have to remedy the situation. Readers have the opportunity to experience vicariously the exhilaration that results when male sexual violence is controlled and finally defeated. The measures taken to achieve this tend to be drastic and the fictions can work to free readers from conditioned compassion, allowing explorations of feelings around this most intense site of struggle between the sexes. In this sense, the fictions might have the power to contribute to social transformation. As Valerie Walkerdine has suggested, 'If wish-fulfilment through fantasy is an important device for working through conflict, then resolutions will have to be engaged with, to create possible paths for action' (p183).

Part of the tradition associated with the genre has undoubtedly been the belief, expressed by both writers and readers, that such imaginative literature will make a difference. As long ago as 1910, in *Our Androcentric Culture*, Gilman expressed the conviction that 'The makers of books are the makers of thoughts and feelings' (pp18–22).

More recently, Carol Farley Kessler has written about her concept of such literature as 'cultural work', as a socially transformative activity and has suggested that 'instead of abstract ideas, fiction presents to our imaginations concrete possibilities that we may not have realised. It can incite us to actualize these ideas in our real lives; thus the fiction functions as a model' (p6).

Daphne Patai sees the literature of imagined worlds as clarifying our vision, 'the way in which Utopias estrange us from our present and thereby allow us to see it more clearly' (pp150–51).

Joanna Russ ends *The Female Man* with an eloquent direct address to her 'little book':

> ...recite yourself to all who will listen; stay hopeful and wise...Do not get glum when you are no longer understood, little book. Do not curse your fate. Do not reach up from readers' laps and punch the readers' noses.
>
> Rejoice, little book.
>
> For on that day, we will be free (pp213–14).

That day has clearly not come and we are clearly not yet free. Such 'little book[s]' still have a lot to say, but, as I earlier indicated, lesbian writers have rarely used this genre in the 1990s. Is there really no vision about changing the world any more? This focus in the late 1990s on individualism and lifestylism in lesbian consciousness, together with a political readiness to welcome, to party with and even to sleep with men, amounts to nothing more than a retreat to an ancient order: heterosexuality. The 'political defiance inherent in utopias' does not serve this politics well. The need for visionary lesbian fiction has never been greater.

REFERENCES

Novels

Charnas, Suzy McKee (1978), *Motherlines*, Berkley Books, New York, 1981 edn; with *Walk to the End of the World*, The Women's Press, London, 1989

Forbes, Caroline, 'London Fields' in *The Needle on Full*, Onlywomen Press, London, 1985

Forrest, Katherine V. (1984), *Daughters of a Coral Dawn*, The Women's Press, London, 1993 edn

Gearhart, Sally Miller (1979), *The Wanderground*, The Women's Press, London, 1985 edn

Gilman, Charlotte Perkins (1915), *Herland*, The Women's Press, London, 1979 edn

Livia, Anna, *Bulldozer Rising*, Onlywomen Press, London, 1987

Russ, Joanna (1975), *The Female Man*, The Women's Press, London, 1989

Other References

Andermahr, Sonya, 'The Worlds of Lesbian/Feminist Science Fiction', in Gabriele Griffin, ed, *Outwrite: Lesbianism and Popular Culture*, Pluto Press, London, 1993

Donawerth, Jane and Carol Kolmerten, *Utopian and Science Fiction by Women: Worlds of Difference*, Liverpool University Press, Liverpool, 1994

Frye, Marilyn (1977), 'Some Reflections on Separatism and Power', in Sarah Lucia Hoagland and Julia Penelope, eds, *For Lesbians Only: A Separatist Anthology*, Onlywomen Press, London, 1988 edn

Gilman, Charlotte Perkins, article in *The Forerunner*, Vol 5, No 5 (February, 1910) New York, pp18–22

Kessler, Carol Farley, *Charlotte Perkins Gilman: Her Progress Towards Utopia*, Liverpool University Press, Liverpool, 1985

Munt, Sally, ed, *New Lesbian Criticism: Literary and Cultural Readings*, Harvester Wheatsheaf, Hemel Hempstead, 1992

Palmer, Paulina, *Contemporary Lesbian Writing: Dreams, Desires, Difference*, Open University Press, Buckingham, 1993

Patai, Daphne, 'Beyond Defensiveness: Feminist Research Strategies', in Masheen Barr and Nicholas D. Smith, eds, *Women and Utopia: Critical Interpretations*, University Press of America, Lanham, MD, 1983

Pfaelzar, Jean, *The Utopian Novel in America 1886–1898: The Politics of Form*, University of Pittsburgh Press, Pittsburgh, 1984

Rosenfelt, Deborah, 'Feminism, Postfeminism and Contemporary Women's Fiction', in *Tradition and the Talents of Women*, Florence Howe, ed, University of Illinois Press, Urbana, 1991

Walkerdine, Valerie, 'Some Day My Prince Will Come: Young Girls and the Preparation for Adolescent Sexuality', in Angela McRobbie and Mica Nava, eds, *Gender and Generation*, Macmillan, New York, 1984

Wittig, Monique (1980), *The Straight Mind*, Harvester Wheatsheaf, London, 1992 edn

Zimmerman, Bonnie (1990), *The Safe Sea of Women: Lesbian Fiction 1969–1989*, Onlywomen Press, London, 1992 edn

NOTES

1 While Charnas does not apparently identify as a lesbian, she writes within a lesbian framework and, crucially for this chapter, offers an incisive critique of heterosexuality in line with radical lesbian feminist theory. See also Zimmerman's comment in *The Safe Sea of Women*: 'To all these writers, the word "lesbian" represented a point of view, or mode of interpretation, rather than a sexual behaviour or innate identity . . . during the 70s and early 80s the meaning of the word "lesbian" was profoundly influenced by feminist politics and ideology' (pp11–12).

2 A front-page report in the *Guardian* on 24 June 1997 revealed that Newnham College, Cambridge University's sole remaining women-only college, had, unknown to most people connected with the college, appointed a transsexual physicist to a post there, despite a 126-year-old statute

protecting the college's women-only status.
3 This happened with the women's walking group Hiking Dykes in the early 1990s.
4 Justice for Women campaigns against male violence and for the release from prison of women convicted of killing violent husbands and male partners in self-defence or in reaction to extreme provocation. The group has argued persuasively to change perceptions of what 'premeditation' means in the cases of such women, likely to be physically less strong than their abusive partners. Women such as Kiranjit Ahluwalia and Emma Humphreys were supported in prison by members of the campaign and finally released, largely due to the activism of Justice for Women and Southall Black Sisters.

GOOD LESBIANS, BAD MEN AND HAPPY ENDINGS[1]

Elaine Hutton

Lesbian feminist thrillers and detective novels are part of the staple diet of lesbian readers. Consuming them is one of the things lesbians do in bed, on holiday and when other more pressing tasks call. They have a huge readership and are reviewed regularly in lesbian and other media. The genre has been analysed consistently in books about lesbian writing and culture, in terms of its subversive properties and the autonomous and independent nature of the detective characters. In the late 1990s, it seems to have become *the* predominant vehicle for lesbian fictional expression.

In surveys of lesbian literature (not just detective fiction) from the 1970s and 1980s there is a consensus that such literature arose out of the women's movement. The lesbian novels of the time engaged with, and were a voice for, the struggle to overthrow the patriarchy and create a new world, free from male oppression. These surveys emphasise that in the early novels a shared feminist vision existed. The classics of lesbian detective fiction tended to be part of this predominant vision. For instance, Barbara Wilson's *Murder in the Collective* (1984) and *Sisters of the Road* (1986) dealt with masculinity and male violence. The devastating effects of sexual abuse were exposed in Katherine V. Forrest's *Murder at the Nightwood Bar* (1987). The horrors of sexual harassment were tackled in

Forrest's *Amateur City* (1984) and Valerie Miner's *Murder in the English Department* (1982). As a contrast to the dangers of relationships with men, coming-out stories were sometimes part of the plot – Barbara Wilson's Pam Nilsen, Sarah Dreher's Gwen (lover of Stoner McTavish). An inspiring feature of these novels, which reflected the mood of the time, was the solidarity and friendship among the women. Women's resistance too was a very important quality. Men sometimes got their comeuppance in wonderful ways. Harasser Angus Murchie had his most humiliating moment as a corpse. Abuser Roland Quillin met his demise by being poisoned, tied to the steering wheel of his car by his wife's brassière and incinerated. (Mrs Quillin, executioner and former collusive mother, was embarrassed at appearing in the police station without her bra.) Bryan Oxnard, violent husband of Gwen, simply disappeared over a precipice.[2]

From the mid-1980s onwards the lesbian feminist community lost its consensus, as has been extensively documented and directly experienced by feminist activists. The conservative backlash spawned the New Lesbian, dedicated to lifestyle, integration with gay men and conservation of heterosexual values, and losing the connection with feminism with its analysis of male power and heterosexuality. Lesbian detective fiction splintered too and now reflects a multitude of different images of lesbians and messages about what it means to be a lesbian. The plots are not so straightforward now either, in terms of their political perspectives. In her ground-breaking survey of lesbian fiction (covering the period 1969–89), Bonnie Zimmerman pointed out that 'in certain ways [it] resembles a popular genre...It is molded by specific conventions and formulas...[M]ost lesbian novels require good lesbians, bad men, and happy endings' (p20). She was specifically referring to the pressure writers experienced from the lesbian feminist community throughout this period to produce 'politically correct' novels (which she called a lesbian version of 'socialist realism' [p19]), sometimes at the expense of complexity of character and style. While partially agreeing with her analysis (though of course it doesn't have to be either/or – at best, our writers might achieve both), I must admit to a sneaking sympathy with the formula, if it means the novelist writes from a radical feminist perspective. If challenging and resisting the patriarchy, imagining ourselves into a world where oppression of women has ended and concerning ourselves with lesbian ethics are the stuff of lesbian novelists, all the better. A sloppy political framework and compromised feminism detracts from my pleasure in a lesbian novel almost as much as bland characterisation or predictable narrative, as there are so few opportunities for radical lesbians to enjoy positive representations of ourselves. However, because lesbian crime fiction has picked up on the more fashionable and visible trends within the lesbian community, it can be frustrating to the feminist reader, even if sometimes more satisfying as 'art'.[3]

In this chapter, I discuss a number of the more recent lesbian detective and thriller novels, looking at questions such as: where do the writers locate themselves in relation to feminism? What kind of lesbians and lesbian community are represented? What position do men occupy in the novels? I consider whether the writers have continued the tradition of feminist writing, to what extent they are influenced by the debates, conflicts and confusions within the lesbian community, and if they reflect the current dominant trends or embody a feminist vision.

They Came to an Impasse: Mary Wings and Ellen Hart

Mary Wings is one of the enduring lesbian thriller writers. Marketed from the beginning as an inheritor of the Raymond Chandler tradition, with 'spare witty prose as hard-boiled as the boys', she has written five novels over an eleven-year span, 1986–97. In her *She Came . . .* series of four novels to date, poverty, urban decay, street violence and other evils of advanced capitalism come under her scrutiny. Her relationship with feminism is more ambiguous.

Her tough dyke detective, Emma Victor, appears on the surface to be a 'liberated' contemporary female counterpart to Philip Marlowe, with her stylish outfits, witty one-liners and propensity for ogling and bedding the women (babes?) she investigates. True to the heritage of thrillers, Emma is a solitary individual, mostly operating alone, except for her friend Rose, who occasionally comes to her rescue.

In the *She Came...* novels, set in Boston and San Francisco, Wings has chosen to reflect the dominant culture – that is, lesbian feminism in the earlier novels and the more conservative lesgay scene in the later ones. Emma fits into this changing social context, taking part in mass meetings fighting cuts to women's services and doing publicity for a women's benefit concert 'against domestic desperation' in the first two books; on the VIP table for a Lesbian and Gay Archive fund-raising dinner and part of the crowd at a Lesbian and Gay Film Festival in the third and fourth. The sleuth's relationship to the changing communities depicted gives some clue to her author's intentions, and to where she stands in relation to feminism.

In the first novel, *She Came Too Late* (1986) feminism functions as no more than a backdrop. The dilemmas and debates which drive the narrative, about state co-option of feminism and reproductive technology, are not engaged with; they merely provide the flavour. Wings' attitude to services for women is curiously glib: Emma's lover says to her, 'The Hotline job has you bored to tears...It's not in your character to do social work' (p112). Institutionalised femicide (systematic killing of women) gets a light-hearted treatment in the following exchange, where Emma is talking to her friend Jonell. Jonell starts the conversation:

'They're developing technology to ensure a male offspring...I mean female infanticide in China, India, who knows, Indiana. What a great solution, "No need to off the baby bundled in pink, just use the handy XY condom and keep the pants in power."'

'Please, stop.' ...

'I think you don't take it seriously enough,' Jonell said.

'And I think you're taking it too seriously. Come on, this is a party, let's have fun' (p61).

In relation to the various settings, Emma is a shadowy and sometimes chameleon-like figure who appears to take on the characteristics of whatever social group she is currently part of. As one character says, 'Anyway, keep an eye out for our investigative moth, you guys. She's a tall babe, salt and pepper hair, walks fast. She doesn't say a lot but kinda lurks around in the shadows' (She Came to the Castro, p177).

This persona forms a narrative function whereby Emma is able to solve the mystery by her observational powers and interventions. At the same time it allows her to remain an outsider in the sense of being a critical and often amused observer of the shifting social milieux and movements, be they women's activism, therapy, new age religion or lesbian careerism. Emma, ironically detached, seems to fulfil the function of author's mouthpiece, as the action takes place through her perspective, and very little irony is directed against her.

Paradoxically, the fact that Wings always chooses to reflect the most visible lesbian culture in her Emma Victor novels means that the third, She Came by the Book (1995), appears more radical than its predecessors. This novel is lodged very firmly in the mid-1990s, with all that that entails. By this time, we had moved far from the certainties of a unitary lesbian feminist identity, and authors of lesbian literature were left in the position of having to make a choice about what kind of lesbians and lesbian community they portrayed. At first sight, the book is as fashionable as its characters, in reflecting the politics of diversity and integration that had taken hold by this time. However, Wings seems more critical than might at first appear of the politics of assimilation, though this may be because of the one constant in the shifting political scene, the satiric narrator. The portrayal of Emma is inconsistent at times, though, as she subscribes to certain values with the apparent endorsement of her creator.

Wings creates two kinds of lesbians: the affluent, power-dressing, lipsticked counterparts to the gay men, and the marginalised, poverty-stricken streetwise kids. Lesbian feminists are completely absent from the book. The closest we come to feminist activism are the 'Lesbian Revengers', who rate nothing more than a mention. The only radical woman represented is a former revolutionary, living underground. She has survived by becoming a 'man', a female to male transsexual.

The characters, who inhabit a world where individualism and materialism are all-important, are treacherous and manipulative. The couples' counsellor Deborah Dunton 'had the kind of movable boundaries that caused wars between countries. Between dykes it was disaster' (p40). The executive director of the Archive, Tracy Port, engineers the humiliation of the black woman keynote speaker at the dinner and is shown to have invited her 'to add a little color' (p31). The lesbians routinely betray each other in their relationships.

In earlier feminist novels of the 1980s, the patriarchal order was often overtly challenged by means of a male aggressor being murdered by a woman. In the present, where fighting the patriarchy is a contested strategy among lesbians, and admiration and love of gay men is supposedly rampant, the rather subtle storyline appears uncompromising in the judgement it makes on queer politics. All three victims of murder here are lesbians, killed by the male lover of a prominent gay man to protect his own position. These assimilated lesbians are seen to operate in a patriarchal, heterosexual framework. One is sleeping with the prominent gay man. As soon as they get in the way of the men, or threaten men, they are expendable. The narrative suggests, then, that Wings is critical of lesbian and gay political alliances. Not only do these alliances leave men firmly in power, but they endanger women's lives!

The characterisation of Emma Victor, however, is more ambiguous. (This is where I, as a reader, start to feel frustrated.) Initially there are some clues that Emma is not entirely at ease with the world she inhabits. The ubiquitous little black dress is an amusing signifier of this. Emma buys this frock as a present for her lover, but ends up wearing it to the fund-raising dinner instead of the intended tuxedo. So what began as 'just the ticket for Frances' lovely, compact body'...'A perfect fit' (p17) continues as a symbol of discomfort on Emma's body. Emma is almost six feet tall and has hairy legs. 'The elasticised minidress clung uncomfortably to [her] body...' (p25). To go with the dress she had to wear tights, which caused her to '[hop] with the odd step that the low crotch gave [her]' (p22).

At the dinner, she comes face to face with the bisexual yuppie, Tracy, wearing the *same dress*. This scene, as classic as the little black frock, is exploited to comic effect: 'Tracy turned around, looking me up and down, her eyes noting the unshaved legs, the inappropriate shoes, the barely decent way the dress clung to my fuller, taller, figure. "Emma, you're a picture!" she said, and then she turned around to show me how it should be done' (p6).

The opening sentence of the Prologue had Emma reflecting that Tracy looked better than herself in the dress, even as she was dying at Emma's feet. This caricature of sartorial rivalry between women prepares us for criticism of the new breed of femme, sexualised lesbians. Stylish, perfectly dressed lesbians are a feature of all the *She Came*...novels. The author's distancing, and her ironic treatment of Emma, is a departure. Nevertheless, they provide an ambiguous message. Emma thought this ridiculous garment would enhance her lover's body and, ultimately, the comedy comes from a butch presuming to wear a femme garment. Emma is a figure of fun because of her bulk, size and inability to mince. The little black dress still rules OK. There is no ultimate challenge to constructed femininity.

There are other inconsistent aspects to the portrayal of

Emma which leave the reader puzzled as to where Wings ultimately stands. Emma is seen to choose the values of the young body-pierced underclass of lesbians who hang out at Red Dora's café.

> While the lesbian career women were still accenting the hollow of their cheekbones with clown-like blusher, women at Red Dora's had shaved their heads and got remarkable tattoos...Red Dora girls wore their wealth on their faces, in your face, and not stored in a lockbox or stock portfolio. The women at Red Dora's had become beautiful to me (p88).

However, she is never critical of the masochism and exploitation of their bodies. When Emma has her nose pierced to gain information, Gurl Jesus is in the booth next door, crying out in pain. She was having her labia pierced – six times. There is no recognition that piercing and tattooing might be self-mutilation. Instead, through Emma, the author seems to offer these examples of 'transgression' as the only alternative to the co-opted lesbians and gays. Rather than an acknowledgement of the radical feminist critique of sado-masochism, there is an admiring endorsement of the 'multiple piercing' and tattooing of the 'young dyke hides in San Francisco' (p87). Earlier in the novel, Emma observes that her friend Rose has a new 'Rose' tattoo, and berates the unaware masses: 'Few people knew that her entire back was wallpapered. A lot of people only saw that Rose was paralysed from the waist down' (p37). Emma seems to be saying that Rose makes herself less disabled and more (attractively) like other lesbians by mutilating her body with tattoos.

In *She Came to the Castro*, Emma hangs out with the same sort of crowd. She identifies with the gay men, calling them 'my people'. However, the threat of male violence is more pronounced than in the previous book. In the Castro Theatre scenes, the sheer physical presence of men spills into the author's portrayal. The reader feels physically overwhelmed by the profusion of buttocks and smelly armpits. 'The floor was a chaos of maleness, the smell of leather, perspiration, panic and pre-ejaculate, filled the air' [p224].) Emma seems to find them physically repulsive even if they are 'her people'.

Ultimately, it is difficult to decide where Wings stands, whether in relation to feminism, queer politics, men or anything else, as she captures the foibles of diverse social movements with ironic detachment through the voice of her detective. The only consistency is Emma, witty, independent and brave, with one-liners the reader dreams of. Maybe we can forgive Wings her lack of conviction in the face of her subversive dyke detective, even though we're not finally sure what she is subverting.

Ellen Hart is another American novelist who has produced a series, portraying detective-cum-restaurant owner Jane Lawless and her theatre director friend, Cordelia Thorn. The lesbians depicted are late-thirtyish to forty-something, wealthy, successful and mainstream; emphasis is placed on their comfortable, tasteful houses and blooming, often artistic, careers. Jane sometimes calls on her prominent lawyer father for help in her investigations. There is no sense, as in Wings' novels, of some lesbians moving into the professional classes at the expense of their integrity or of others'; the values here are solidly bourgeois. The amateur detective, Jane, in the tradition of earlier women's detective fiction, sometimes adopts a Miss Marple role by being an irritant to the police.

'And Ms Lawless, one more thing. I know in the past you've tried to lend the police a hand.'...

'Why, Detective Trevelyan, I didn't think you'd remember how easily I cleared up that little business at the sorority two years ago. It's so nice to be appreciated...' (*Stage Fright*, p25).

Hart provides an insight into the workings of male power and an analysis of patriarchy through her novels. However, this is compromised to some extent, as the following two glimpses into Jane's thought processes (presented without irony) indicate. Jane and Cordelia move in an arty, theatrical crowd and have male friends. In *A Small Sacrifice* (1994), Jane reflects that Cordelia loved make-up and 'never tried to squelch a natural inclination for a political reason'. Throughout the 'seventies and eighties, she'd steadfastly worn her make-up, even though she got some nasty looks from women who felt she was a sell-out to the patriarchy.' Jane decides that her friend did 'what came naturally. No matter who it annoyed' (p118). This extraordinary little episode gives a hint of Hart's attitude to the feminist project of deconstructing femininity, and, for that matter, her misunderstanding of its social construction, as she appears to attribute the donning of blush, eyeliner or lipstick to something essentially female in Cordelia's personality. And in *Faint Praise* (1995), in the context of disliking a heterosexual friend's boyfriend, Jane ponders defensively that she 'found lots of men both attractive and great company' (p152). The danger of such a placatory viewpoint, of course, is that the feminism is diluted, which is exactly what happens. Hart's novels are shot through with contradictions as a result of not being clear about her political framework.

Nevertheless, *Stage Fright* (1992) is clearly written from a feminist perspective. A critique of the family is central to the plot. The role of playwright Gaylord Werness as the conscience of the 1960s (he made his name writing against the Vietnam War and berating America as a 'violent nation') is juxtaposed against his position and role in his family. Jane's Aunt Beryl reflects, 'His longish white hair and beard made her think of an Old Testament patriarch' (p57). Cordelia describes him as 'a degenerate Santa Claus' (p109).

The novel's opening scenes focus on the staging of a play written by Gaylord's eldest daughter, Antonia, herself a respected playwright. Her play 'revolves around the women in...one family...The grandmother, the mother and the daughter' (p23). 'The difference in [the women's] life experiences and expectations form the basis for the story' (p24). It emerges gradually that Antonia had written the play to avenge her mother and sister. The only view we have of the mother is through her husband, who refers to her in sentimental terms as 'not strong' and 'with emotional problems' (p90). Gaylord had her institutionalised in the early 1960s, at the height not only of his reputation but also, we realise as the plot unfolds, his abusive terrorising actions towards his two younger children.

Antonia's play is titled *Audience for a Bride Doll* and part of the set are six large 'bride dolls dressed appropriately for their particular era' (pp23–4). However, the title of this play, and indeed the title of the novel, *Stage Fright*, are jointly transformed into a feminist joke. Gaylord's son Torald dies when being resisted by a young woman he tries to assault on the stage set, by being impaled on a huge steel fork held by the seven-foot bride. Gaylord himself is finally humiliated and forced to acknowledge his abusive actions in two separate incidents which show the women he damaged fighting back.

However, there is a strand running through the novel where various characters speculate on the nature of evil and whether Gaylord was truly evil, a question which is left unresolved. This has the effect of slightly undermining the feminism of the novel, as does the conclusion Jane and Cordelia draw, that Torald 'was a victim just like everyone else' (p260). The evidence of the novel is against this view. Most of the women are depicted as strong survivors and *resisters* who support each other, while the men are portrayed variously as weak, controlling, collusive and petulant. In short, constructed masculinity is accurately delineated and its echoes reverberate far beyond the central patriarch.

Both son and daughter were abused by Gaylord, but whereas the daughter survives and fights back, the son is contemptuous of his wife, violent towards women and a rapist. There are many other instances throughout the novel of men using personal and institutionalised power against women. Jane's own father, Raymond, had been hired by Gaylord to get Torald off the rape charge. There are obvious parallels, in the antagonistic relationship between Jane's father and aunt, with the primary plot, as Raymond attempts to control his family and divide the women. Billy Brewster, the golden-haired heir to the theatrical dynasty, colludes with Gaylord. There are sinister echoes of Gaylord's behaviour in Billy's attempt to medicalise Erin (and he is one of the *nice* men): '"Maybe [you] should see a doctor...Come on, why don't you lie down...I'll have him come in and take a look at you"' (p202).

Hart's irreverent attitude to masculinity is evident in the following exchange between Antonia and a minor character, Victor. The latter's determination to claim the long-lost Billy as his son comically underlines the patriarchal obsession with ownership of people, a theme replayed throughout the novel.

'Is it me? Have I done something to upset you?'
She put her hand to her mouth to stop herself from laughing out loud. He had *such* a talent for being obtuse – for saying the exact wrong thing. It was almost getting to be a joke.
'Of course it's you.'
'Why? What?'
A small giggle leaked out. 'Everything' (pp188–9).

But in spite of the convincing range of portraits of nice and nasty men who underneath are still men, the novel ends with the question again of whether 'evil [can be] embodied in a person' (p261). By leaving us with the thought that 'evil' is individualised into one bad man, whose actions have reverberative effects on lots of other people, the feminist critique of socially constructed masculinity is weakened. Though a feminist perspective clearly infuses both plot and characterisation, the ultimate message seems to impose a different interpretation, as it reduces the narrative to a question of conventional morality, with the forces of good winning out over evil.

Nice Men?

However, the apparent withdrawal from a critique of masculinity paves the way for Hart's next novel, *A Small Sacrifice* (1994). This is about a group of friends of Cordelia's from university drama school days. They are now '40 somethings' who all 'love' each other deeply. As with the previous novel, the plot turns on masculinity, but here it is a tamed, affectionately regarded attribute. Central to the story is a competition between two of the (male) friends that practically ruins their lives. There is no critique of this, more a 'boys will be boys' indulgence, as the following exchange between Jane and Cordelia demonstrates.

'... Couldn't wait to test their mettle.'
  'They were idiots!'
  'Of course they were. But they were young and – '
  'Full of testosterone' (p264).

As we advanced further into the 1990s, the pressure from this more conservative era to embrace masculinity rather than criticise it was reflected in lesbian writing. In this particular novel the men are mates, indistinguishable from the women characters in terms of their behaviour and interactions with the women (a case of literature not reflecting life). But although they are all – married, single, straight or gay – portrayed superficially as having equality, as regards economic situation and status: for instance, the lesbian co-parent (the only lesbian apart from Cordelia) is shown to be a drunkard, incapable of caring for her dead lover's daughter. Ultimately, this young woman goes to live with the only married couple in the group.

The saving grace for me in this (intriguingly gripping) thriller is that Cordelia drafts in Jane to help her solve the mystery. Evidently her mixed bag of dear friends aren't sustenance enough.

And Bad Women

Robber's Wine (1996) resembles *Stage Fright* in that it not only highlights women's experience of domestic violence but shows women fighting back. As in the earlier novel, a family is central to the plot. This family, though, is headed by several generations of independent women who have exacted revenge on powerful, exploitative men and/or lived as single parents. Abusive, violent and dangerous men are a leitmotif. Hart is adept at painting strong women characters and showing the forces ranged against them living under patriarchy. '"Until the day she died, [Fanny] was scared to death of that man. She passed that fear on to Belle"' (p264).

Hart's analysis of domestic violence and its effect on a particular woman – loss of confidence, self-blaming, feelings of terrible isolation, attempts to placate the violent man – is horribly accurate. Unfortunately, though, she shows little understanding of women who kill violent men, and ultimately appears to have no empathy with women who are victims of male violence. This is evident from her characterisation of the woman later in the book, and the role assigned to the investigator, Jane, who very decisively turns out *not* to be lawless. The victim/survivor is portrayed as a potential multiple killer, likely to murder anyone who would threaten her security, whereas it is well documented that women who kill violent men do so for their own survival and are unlikely to kill again.

Jane's stance in this particular novel is extremely problematic. Cordelia realises it is better to let sleeping dogs (or dead men) lie, even if one of the violent men is falsely assumed by the police to have murdered the other.

Cordelia whistled. '... That's great news!'
    'But it's not right!' said Jane, erupting from the couch...
    '... If the police found proof, that's good enough for me. This is the best news we could get, Janey. It means the entire Dumont clan is innocent.'
    'But it's wrong,' said Jane... 'Pfeifer had nothing to do with Quinn's death...' (p269).

Jane's concept of right and wrong here is firmly rooted in

patriarchal law and justice. It does not allow mitigating circumstances, like male violence, which has led, in one instance, to years of violent abuse, and in the other, to a woman's death. Jane is not unaware of the attitude the police are likely to take to women fighting back either, as in *Stage Fright* the policeman Trevelyan had attempted to pin a murder charge on her, saying, '"Maybe he forced himself on you and you wanted revenge. Sure. We've been warned to watch for things like that. What with the Willy Smith rape trial in Florida and that Anita Hill thing, women don't trust the system any more. I can tie you to this, *I know I can*"' (p119).

Incredibly, in spite of knowing how the police discriminate against women, in *Robber's Wine* Jane assists them in laying a trap for the woman she (rightly) suspects of Quinn's murder. The novel ends with the pregnant woman facing the prospect of a long prison sentence, and hoping her baby doesn't 'grow up to be like [her]' (p287). Jane, who has caused her to be arrested, thinks of her as 'tragic' and doesn't reassure her.

This is a far cry from the solidarity between women of earlier feminist detective novels. In Valerie Miner's *Murder in the English Department*, Nan Weaver was prepared to keep silent, conceal evidence and go to prison to protect a student who had murdered her sexual harasser, because 'she was another woman... She needed help' (p148). In Barbara Wilson's *Murder in the Collective*, three women protect their friend who has murdered her dangerous ex-husband. As one of them reflects, '[June] hadn't pursued Zee like a detective, she'd confronted her like a woman and stayed to comfort her like a friend.' The two women amateur investigators agree that she can't go to prison: 'The weapon's gone, they've got nothing on you other than that you married him... You've got too many things to do to be spending your life in prison' (p179).

While I thoroughly enjoy Ellen Hart's novels for their portrayal of strong women and women's friendship, and their inventive plots, I feel they stray at times, unwittingly perhaps, into the earlier conservative genre of crime fiction, rather than continuing the more radical tradition of feminist literature.

Bad Lesbians

Two novels whose plots centre on relationships between women, one dealing with a collective and the other with individual 'lover' relationships, are American Sarah Dreher's *Bad Company* (1995) and Mary Wings' *Divine Victim* (1992). *Bad Company* positions itself very firmly within the feminist tradition of earlier lesbian literature. However, it is modified by the 1990s context in the sense that, by now, writers are acknowledging that women do not always get on or treat each other well: 'Like the rest of her generation, Stoner had learned – with a fair amount of pain – that being women didn't mean you'd exchanged penises for haloes' (p27). Both novels feature sadistic women, but their cruelty is assigned different motivations by each author. One critic thinks the portrayal of Ilona in *Divine Victim* (a novel inspired by Daphne du Maurier's *Rebecca*) might be criticised 'on the grounds that it is sensational and panders to the current fascination with SM' (Palmer, p76). Wings' 1992 account of writing the book, 'Rebecca Redux', certainly supports this view, as she talks about 'a twentieth-century gothic for queers' (p13), Rebecca being 'every woman's symbol of forbidden sexuality' (p17), and 'releasing the trapped female desire that beckons so in *Rebecca*' (p31). But the impression the novel makes is very different. Wings talks in the same lecture of keeping the Gothic formula where 'the past informs the present' (p31), and this is the key to the novel's radicalism.

The setting of *Bad Company* is an upmarket women-only holiday inn. Ironically, because of the attacks on, and shifts away from, feminism, it seems almost dated, in that the troubles Dreher's Stoner McTavish has been invited to sort out are occurring in a 'wimmin's amateur theatre group' (p1) which not only works collectively, with the women giving up free time to rehearse, but also provides its own technical support – sound and lighting women, carpenters and decorators (a contrast to the professional theatre crowd who form the backdrop to Ellen Hart's novels). The group also has collective meetings to 'process its issues', though these are treated with some irony by the author.

There are similarities with Wings' novel of the same year (*She Came by the Book*). Dreher is clearly opposed to the materialism and professionalism of post-feminist 'luppies'. Initially Stoner has reservations about taking on the case, partly because of

'The people who probably go there ... well, sometimes I have a hard time with Yuppie Dykes in high heels.'

'Nobody calls them Yuppies any more. These are the "nineties".' (p4)

However, Dreher is more explicit than Wings about what has been lost. Stoner, as well as having instantly recognisable lesbian feminist characteristics such as a liking for jeans, shirts and boots and a dislike of Norman Mailer, has a recognisable sense of historical yearning. Gwen observes, '"[You have] that Remembering the Women's Movement look, kind of sad and disillusioned"' (p27). Stoner cogitates, 'The younger women looked at the old revolutionaries as dinosaurs, and cringed at the use of the word Feminism. Even lesbians, that ever-contentious tribe, seemed to be satisfied to call themselves "gay women," and spend their evenings at gender-free dances' (pp59–60).

The novel is a deliberate rebuttal of the depoliticised lifestyle expression of lesbianism; a conscious harking back to the values of the early women's movement. This becomes more obvious when we discover that the perpetrator of the mischief, the Destroyer Within, is the 'nineties-type' Yuppie owner of the hotel, whose stated motive for destroying the company was that 'it went collective'.

Dreher is not uncritical of sisterhood. She parodies some of its manifestations, such as matriarchal rituals. For instance, the ritual that occurs here is called a 'Bitching

Ceremony', and while it is happening Stoner is involved in an action-packed life-threatening fight with the villain, while the rest of the women, oblivious in their healing circle, chant the name of numerous goddesses to help them solve the problem of (misuse of) power in the collective!

However, enmeshed in the fabric of the book is a sense of historical perspective and solidarity between women. A connection is made through Stoner's name between the first feminist wave ('The Lucy B. Stoners ... were married ladies who kept their maiden names, the way Lucy did' [p94]), (stone) butches and contemporary feminist activists. The two old women who help Stoner in trapping the villain have always been activists. Hope of continuity is set against Stoner's despair about the future of feminism.

Less satisfying to the feminist reader is the motivation attributed to the perpetrator of the problems. She manipulates the women, humiliating them and undermining their confidence, by causing accidents or destructive incidents. This character resembles a 'bad mother' in Agatha Christie's *Appointment with Death* (1938). As in Christie's novel, she calls in Stoner so that she has an extra person to trick: '"I could have destroyed this company with my eyes closed," she explained patiently. "Where's the thrill in that?"' (p231). But Dreher does not go beyond the psychological explanation of the Christie plot, which draws on early Freudian theory about sadism. While this might be understandable to use as a motivation for a character in 1938, when psychology was being popularised, it is surprising, in a feminist novel of the mid-1990s, that problems of power within the women's movement should be explained in individualised, psychological terms.[4]

A radical feminist analysis maintains that, as masculinity is constructed in a particular way, where male violence is normalised and institutionalised, so is femininity, where women are socialised to compete and betray each other. Developing a code of ethics and a sense of solidarity with other women has to be built; these features are not automatically part of women's character. As Stoner rightly observes, we are not angels. Therefore, the symbolic meaning of *Bad Company* – the 1990s Bad Lesbian, representative of anti-feminist values, attempting to destroy the co-operative spirit of collective feminism – speaks with more *political* meaning than a psychological explanation of individual pathology.

The cruelty perpetrated by Ilona in *Divine Victim* is given a political context. To me, the novel reflects feminist values much more unambiguously than the *She Came*...series. Wings said of it in 'Rebecca Redux', 'I have updated the lesbian gothic to current standards of fear and terror. The fear of being the victim. The terror of lost selfhood in being complicit in a victim/abuser relationship and trapped in a terrible dynamic!' (p32). This statement indicates that she is not flirting with sado-masochism, although, given the current ideological back-lash where it is being increasingly asserted that abuse by women is a large hidden problem, she is perhaps using terms too loosely.

The story is woven tantalisingly around the Daphne du Maurier thriller *Rebecca* (and the Hitchcock film version of the same, as Wings makes clear in her account). In spite of the grim subject matter, Wings' comic skills are to the fore, with pungent contemporary updates to the original story. An ice-climbing, leisure-wearing softball enthusiast is the lesbian version of the boring Max de Winter; a Catholic fundamentalist homophobe replaces house-keeper Mrs Danvers but retains the aura of obsessive menace. Unlike the original, Wings' narrator is not a passive victim, her fight-back to regain her self-respect becoming the surprising plot twist at the end (although it is a hollow victory).

The yearning obsession of Du Maurier's narrator with the eponymous Rebecca is wonderfully parodied. In *Divine Victim*, while the lesbian narrator researches the story of the mysterious dead ex-nun Rebecca, her discoveries prompt flashbacks to her relationship with a glamorous, sadistic art historian. The pathetic and sometimes inadvertent attempts of Du Maurier's narrator to emulate the beautiful Rebecca are hilariously transformed by Wings into a power struggle between lovers, as Ilona, the art historian, attempts to change the narrator to her specifications:

> 'Sweetheart,' she would chide me...
> My clothes were wrong, my hands flew about when I spoke, my voice, she said, sounded like braying. But I was speaking German, a language that belonged to someone else, I said. It didn't matter. Braying was braying.
> She took me to the market, where colourful cheap trousers and sweaters could be bought to replace my old garments which I suddenly realised were very American and intrinsically unattractive' (p34).

The scenes between Ilona and the narrator are painful to read. Nevertheless, lots of lesbians will recognise the conflicts – the bickering on holiday about whether to do the washing first or go into town, the ruined birthday, the capitulations and appeasements. Even the legendary lesbian fixation on cats is turned to Gothic horror, as the stiff putrefying puss in the campsite becomes a symbol of their diseased relationship. There is an authenticity and power in the descriptions of the women's disintegrating relationship not often captured in other novels about lesbian relationships I have read. There is also a rare glimpse of the pressures caused by work, as one woman's academic career is taking off, while the other's is waning.

However, women's ability to hurt one another is put very firmly within the framework of patriarchy, with its institutions of abusive fathers and Christianity. In the convent subplot, the sanctions against lesbianism administered by the Mother Superior are shown as extreme brutality, if not torture. Significantly, in the Italian holiday scenes, it is the intervention of the two men, 'Moustache' and 'Cockscomb', and their threat of violence, which provokes the final showdown between the women, as the sadistic Ilona colludes with them against her 'lover'. The manner in which the past informs the present is contained in the witty title of the book: women are victims of patriarchy whether they are nuns imprisoned in convents, beautiful academics on holiday in Italy, or en route to a pagan shrine in the middle of the night, in a 7-Eleven store in icy Montana...

When Hens Have Teeth

But in some recent fiction they fight back. Two British novels which specifically reflect the values of feminism are Maggie Kelly's *Burning Issues* (1995) and Manda Scott's *Hen's Teeth* (1996). These are both nearer in spirit to earlier lesbian detective novels, although their ultimate vision is perhaps tempered by the experience of the intervening years. They are not so optimistic about women's ability to survive undamaged.

The narrator in *Burning Issues* has a radical feminist perspective. The title is a timely reminder of feminist priorities and the novel itself a critique of patriarchy, the plot concerned with the pornography industry and the way social policy introduced by the British government throughout the 1980s enables the easy exploitation of vulnerable women (and men). It is a far cry from the normalisation or condoning of pornography evident in some contemporary lesbian detective novels.

Through the array of male characters, masculinity is laid bare and connections are made between all men. While the villains are the murderous pornographers, all the other men are abusive towards, or contemptuous of, women to some degree. Danny, the working-class young offender in the protagonist Mig's writing class, is violent towards the young addict, Mandy, although he defends Mig in a street confrontation against other violent men and helps her at times. Mig's pompous ex-husband treats her like an idiot. While she dearly loves her son, Jack, Mig is clear that he is not an exception. After a typical display of boorishness when he slams out of the house, she hears on the radio that 'a woman had been jailed for life for killing her violent, alcoholic husband. A man had just been given a two-year suspended sentence for strangling his "nagging" wife' (p19). We are left in no doubt as to the links being made in her mind between her son and other men, as well as the institutionalised oppression of women within the family.

A skilfully drawn incident neatly exposes men's socialisation. It also shows the relentless male aggression which permeates women's lives. Mig, feeling guilty about her neglect of Jack (socialisation of mothers is depicted as well), tempts him to stay home with a cooked meal and video of his choice. Predictably, he chooses a violent, pornographic and racist film. After the ensuing row with her son, there is a scene only too familiar to the feminist activist, as Mig confronts the video-shop owners. The wife defends the film – 'It's an adventure' – and calls her husband. In his slippers and jogging bottoms, he threatens Mig, calling her a 'bloody crank' and telling her to bugger off, to the amusement of the other customers. Mig's despondent response is also familiar: 'Not a bad day's work: I'd alienated my partner, been sworn at by a teenage dickhead and been called a crank by a wanker who just happened to own the only late-night small shop for miles' (p30).

The effort needed for women merely to survive under patriarchy, the petty consequences of them retaliating, is beautifully drawn in this low-key scene. There is, however, a wonderful moment to offset it which shows women's resilience, as well as lesbian irreverence and contempt of men: '[W]e were walking along the beach in the first snow flurry of the winter; six of us arm in arm doing a Tiller routine in the freezing sand, the wind flinging salt and snow into our mouths as we sang *our* version of "Stand by Your Man"' (p98, my italics).

Our humour and our rewriting of patriarchal routines *are* what keep us going, and that recognition is one of the strengths of this novel. Mig's impetus to become an investigator arises out of solidarity with other women. She is a political activist who is concerned about what happened to one old woman and what may happen to others. Nevertheless, the ending is realistic, rather than visionary. It is grim; a partial victory. Mig manages to dispatch one dangerous man, survives an attempt on her life (with the help of a pub landlady) and brings some of the villains to justice. Yet the most dangerous man, who has a terrifying understanding of feminists – 'You're the female warrior avenging oppressed womanhood?' (p165) – escapes. The porn network survives; Mig's fear of the ruthless villain lives on in her consciousness. The reader is left with the conviction that, whatever the odds, we have to keep fighting.

This is just what the tough, confident band of young women in Scott's *Hen's Teeth* do. Unlike Mig, they do not consciously identify as feminists. They are professional women: a practising pathologist, an ex-doctor and medical researcher, a computer journalist and so on. They have other skills – carpentry, electrics, computer hacking, abseiling. They show intelligence, initiative and daring in solving the mystery. There is not really a sense of feminist activism; the women are products *of* women's liberation, rather than campaigners *for*. At the same time, the atmosphere of the novel is chillingly patriarchal. The women live in a framework of horrible violence, where they (and their animals) can be tortured if they oppose the male order and murdered for asking questions which expose men making illicit financial gain. Throughout the novel there is a sense of impending threat and danger.

Like *Burning Issues*, the novel exposes abuses of patriarchal rule. One influential entrepreneur, a patron of the arts who runs a farm as an education centre, has built it on 'the blood and body fluids of Glasgow's under-age whores and rent-boys' (p217). The cynical corruption, commodification of people and casual disregard for life of a gang of ruthless men are juxtaposed against the courage of the small group of women who oppose them. The plot wittily interplays the lesbians' complicated relationships with the solving of the crime. Kellen's agreement to take on the role of investigator, at Caroline's request, becomes her way of 'saying goodbye' to her murdered ex-lover, Bridget, and building bridges with Caroline, Bridget's last lover. Kellen's difficulties with her present lover, Jan, and Jan's need 'to talk' are eclipsed by the urgent necessity of solving the crime before the rest of them are endangered. Amusingly, Kellen manages to get the (lesbian) police-woman away from the farm on the night Jan is coming to illegally hack into a computer by the device of claiming Jan is coming to the farm 'to talk'. The policewoman is not fooled but can think of no way of short-circuiting this sacrosanct lesbian imperative. And Jan has agreed to hack only after extracting a promise from Kellen that afterwards they will 'talk'. At the end, there is an uneasy but real community between all the women who didn't speak to various of the others before the plot unwound – Kellen, Caroline, Lee, Jan; more trust of the policewoman, Elspeth; and a seeming acknowledgement from Jan that Kellen's friendship with Lee is as important as their relationship, if not more.

The real community created by resistance – co-operating, taking risks and looking out for each other – is contrasted with the sterility of the conventional lesbian dinner-party scene, with its blandness and gossip.

> I knew all of the rest by sight, so most of them must have known me and I have no doubt that the grapevine had carried the news of my circumstances with its usual efficiency...
>
> Rae Larssen, her perfect hostess instincts tuned to impending conflict, appeared at my side with a fluted glass and a bottle of white Burgundy (p153).

The isolated farmhouse serves as a symbol at the centre of the novel, from which the author neatly overturns the convention of women as passive. The characters are presented as active resisters rather than fearful victims waiting helplessly to be harmed or killed. Kellen describes a daring and dangerous abseiling effort as 'Nerve. It's all a question of nerve' (p95), also a nice reversal of the earlier myth of women with 'nerves'. Scott follows other writers who have used feathered imagery as a metaphor for women,[5] having Kellen observe a merlin killing a wren, as she later tells Jan, 'because it sang. Life can be very unjust at times', to which Jan rejoins, 'Only if you think like a wren.' Kellen acknowledges the 'difference between victim and hunter' and thinks she is 'both probably. It's a very fine dividing line at times' (p252).

All the women in the novel are lesbians. They do overcome their conditioning and resist their fear of becoming victims. The clear message is that they unite by fighting male violence. Two of them, both trained in patriarchal medicine, are badly injured by the men. In a wonderful scene, they cleanse themselves in the healing jet of a waterfall, as (male) antibiotics have not worked – a symbolic sloughing of the 'purulent discharge' of patriarchy. The novel ends with a positive and exhilarating act of retribution, on hogmanay, where one of the women takes justice into her own hands. The danger of doing this is underlined. Even the reader is not let in on the woman's identity.

This novel is an affirmation of lesbian feminist spirit, a reminder of our collective fighting potential. We still have the capacity for changing the world, and some of our thrillers still grasp this feminist vision.

A Happy Ending?

This survey of lesbian crime fiction suggests that there is cause for optimism about the genre. All the novelists discussed are uncompromising about the persistence of male violence. Their independent, resourceful characters recognise the importance of women's friendship and show willing to fight male power. While some of the novels reflect the present more reactionary and liberal context, they indisputably form a link with earlier examples of the genre. They continue, alongside lesbian feminist activism, to be part of the struggle to bring about political change.

REFERENCES

Novels

Dreher, Sarah (1985), *Stoner McTavish*, Pandora Press, 1987 edn; The Women's Press, London 1996

—(1995), *Bad Company*, The Women's Press, London 1996 edn

Forrest, Katherine V. (1984), *Amateur City*, Pandora Press, London, 1987 edn

—, *Murder at the Nightwood Bar*, Pandora Press, London, 1987

Hart, Ellen (1992), *Stage Fright*, The Women's Press, London, 1994 edn

—(1994), *A Small Sacrifice*, The Women's Press, London, 1996 edn

—(1995), *Faint Praise*, The Women's Press, London, 1997 edn

—(1996), *Robber's Wine*, The Women's Press, London, 1997 edn

Kelly, Maggie, *Burning Issues*, Onlywomen Press, London, 1995

Miner, Valerie, *Murder in the English Department*, The Women's Press, London, 1982

Scott, Manda, *Hen's Teeth*, The Women's Press, London, 1996

Wilson, Barbara, *Murder in the Collective*, The Women's Press, London, 1984

—(1986), *Sisters of the Road*, The Women's Press, London, 1987 edn

Wings, Mary, *She Came Too Late*, The Women's Press, London, 1986

—, *She Came in a Flash*, The Women's Press, London, 1988

—, *Divine Victim*, The Women's Press, London, 1992

—, *She Came by the Book*, The Women's Press, London, 1995

—, *She Came to the Castro*, The Women's Press, London, 1997

Other References

Duncker, Patricia, *Sisters and Strangers: An Introduction*

to *Contemporary Feminist Fiction*, Blackwell, Oxford, 1992

Hutton, Elaine, 'The Flight of the Feminist', in Lynne Harne and Elaine Miller, eds, *All The Rage: Reasserting Radical Lesbian Feminism*, The Women's Press, London, 1996

Munt, Sally, *Murder by the Book? Feminism and the Crime Novel*, Routledge, London and New York, 1994

Palmer, Paulina, *Contemporary Lesbian Writing: Dreams, Desire, Difference*, Open University Press, Buckingham, 1993

Wings, Mary (1992), 'Rebecca Redux: Tears on a Lesbian Pillow', in Liz Gibbs, ed, *Daring to Dissent: Lesbian Culture from Margin to Mainstream*, Cassell, London, 1994

Zimmerman, Bonnie (1990), *The Safe Sea of Women: Lesbian Fiction 1969–1989*, Onlywomen Press, London, 1992 edn

NOTES

1 I am indebted to Bonnie Zimmerman for the title.
2 Angus Murchie is a character in *Murder in the English Department*, Roland Quillin in *Murder at the Nightwood Bar* and Bryan Oxnard in *Stoner McTavish*.
3 In a previous article, I suggested that there is an increasing tendency in these novels to embody conservative values and even actively anti-feminist positions, and made the case that the evolution from a feminist to a anti-feminist stance can be traced in certain novelists. (Hutton, pp151–5). Other critics have applauded such novels for their maturity and artistic experimentation.
4 Psychological motivations tend to have a puzzling persistence, even in lesbian feminist novels. In Dreher's first novel, *Stoner McTavish* (1985), the villain is described as 'insane'. In Hart's *Robber's Wine* (1996), the violent husband is said to be 'crazy, certifiable' and 'unstable'. But within the terms of the novels themselves the psychological explanation often sits uneasily.
5 For instance, Pat Barker in *Blow Your House Down*, Virago, London, 1984, used a cental image of a chicken factory and trussed chickens going to their slaughter as a background to a plot in which women are being murdered by a serial killer. Hens with teeth make a welcome change.

CONTRIBUTORS' NOTES

Lynne Harne has taught Women's Studies and Lesbian Studies within the Sociology Department at the University of Westminster as a visiting lecturer for a number of years. She is a long-time feminist activist and doesn't believe that 'feminist academia' is any substitute for feminist campaigning. She has been constantly irritated by representations of lesbian personal relationships in lesbian feminist fiction – hence her motivation to write in this anthology – but would like to stress that she has no pretensions to lesbian literary criticism. She is currently involved in a campaign to stop violent and abusive men having access to children. Her recent publications include *All the Rage* with Elaine Miller (The Women's Press, 1996) and *Valued Families: The Lesbian Mothers' Legal Handbook* with Rights of Women (The Women's Press, 1997).

Vada Hart is a middle-aged, feminist lesbian of working-class origin, living in London. She is a former worker and collective member of the London Lesbian Archive, set up in the 1980s by radical feminists, and has played an active part in the Lesbian History Group.

Elaine Miller is a lesbian and a revolutionary feminist. She was born in 1939 into a mining family in the South Yorkshire coalfield, graduating with a degree in English

Language and Literature from University College London in 1961. A decade later, she discovered lesbian feminism through the women's liberation movement. She was formerly on the Lesbian Archive collective and was active in the planning and organisation of the Lesbian History Group from 1986 to 1995, contributing to the group's book *Not a Passing Phase: Reclaiming Lesbians in History 1840–1985* (The Women's Press, 1989). She has a chapter in Suzanne Raitt, ed, *Volcanoes and Pearl Divers: Essays in Lesbian Feminist Studies* (Onlywomen Press, 1995) and is co-editor with Lynne Harne of *All the Rage: Reasserting Radical Lesbian Feminism* (The Women's Press, 1996). She has written articles and reviews in international feminist journals and has taught on Women's Studies and Literature programmes in further and adult education and in the University of London Extra-Mural Department. She sees teaching and writing as important forms of feminist activism.

Anita Naoko Pilgrim is mixed-heritage Japanese/English, born in Scotland, brought up in Sierra Leone, Thailand, the Cameroons and Somerset, England. She was educated at Whitstone Comprehensive School, Shepton Mallet, Strode College, Street, and King's College, Cambridge. A survivor of childhood sexual abuse, she now leads a happy and fulfilled life. She teaches Social Anthropology and Literature access courses at Birkbeck College and is doing her Ph.D. at Goldsmith's College, University of London, looking at race, sex/gender and sexuality. She has previously published a chapter on black lesbian literature in Valerie Mason-John's *Talking Black* (Cassell, London, 1995) and has written articles for *The Pink Paper*, *Diva*, *Gay Times*, *The Lesbian Review of Books* and *Rugby World*, among others. Her interests include reading, reading and more reading; she also likes cooking, eating, running and single malt whiskies.

Jill Radford is an activist and radical feminist who enjoys reading women's crime fiction. She worked for ten years at

Rights of Women and in 1996 moved to Cleveland, where she is now a Reader in Women's Studies and Criminology at the University of Teesside. She continues to be actively involved in campaigning for justice for women.

Anira Rowanchild is a writer and teacher who lives in Herefordshire. She has published literary criticism, poems and short stories, including in The Women's Press anthology of lesbian feminist stories *Girls Next Door* (1985). She is currently working on a novel about a lesbian's experience of rural life, and a non-fiction work on lesbian autobiography.

Lis Whitelaw is a writer and lecturer who teaches courses in Literature, Women's Studies, Popular Culture and Creative Writing for the Open University and other institutions. In 1990 The Women's Press published her biography *The Life and Rebellious Times of Cicely Hamilton* and she has contributed short stories to anthologies of lesbian feminist fiction. She has written extensively about lesbian fiction, biography and autobiography from a lesbian feminist perspective. She is currently doing research on contemporary feminist writing in Aotearoa/New Zealand.

Rachel Wingfield is a psychotherapist who lives in London. She has been involved in campaigning against violence against women and children for over thirteen years.

FURTHER READING

Novels and Stories Mentioned in Text

Alther, Lisa (1976), *Kinflicks*, Penguin Books,
    Harmondsworth, 1977 edn

—, *Original Sins*, The Women's Press, London, 1981

—(1984), *Other Women*, Penguin Books,
    Harmondsworth, 1985 edn

—, *Bedrock*, Viking, Harmondsworth, 1990

—, *Five Minutes in Heaven*, Penguin Books,
    Harmondsworth, 1995

Arnold, June, *Sister Gin*, Daughters Inc., Vermont, 1975;
    The Women's Press, London, 1979

Burford, Barbara, *The Threshing Floor*, Sheba Feminist
    Publishers, London, 1986

—, 'The Pinstripe Summer', in *The Threshing Floor*

Charnas, Suzy McKee (1978), *Motherlines*, Berkley Books,
    New York, 1981; (with *Walk to the End of the
    World*), The Women's Press, London, 1989

Cooper, Fiona (1998), *Rotary Spokes*, Serpent's Tail,
    London, 1995 edn

—, *Skyhook in the Midnight Sun*, Serpent's Tail, London,
    1994

Donoghue, Emma (1994), *Stir Fry*, Penguin Books,
    Harmondsworth, 1995 edn

—, *Hood*, Hamish Hamilton, Harmondsworth, 1995

Dreher, Sarah (1985), *Stoner McTavish*, Pandora, London,

1987 edn; The Women's Press, London, 1996

—(1995), *Bad Company*, The Women's Press, London, 1996 edn

Drury, Joan M. (1996), *Silent Words*, The Women's Press, London, 1997 edn

Duffy, Maureen (1996), *The Microcosm*, Virago, London, 1989 edn

—(1971), *Love Child*, Virago, London, 1994 edn

—(1991), *Illuminations*, Flamingo, London, 1992 edn

Fairbanks, Tash, *Fearful Symmetry*, Onlywomen Press, London, 1996

Forbes, Caroline, 'London Fields', in *The Needle on Full*, Onlywomen Press, London, 1985

Forrest Katherine V. (1984), *Amateur City*, Pandora, London, 1987 edn

—(1984), *Daughters of a Coral Dawn*, The Women's Press, London, 1993 edn

—, *Murder at the Nightwood Bar*, Pandora, London, 1987

French, Marilyn (1977), *The Women's Room*, Sphere Books, London, 1979 edn

Galford, Ellen, *The Fires of Bride*, The Women's Press, London, 1986

Gearhart, Sally Miller (1979), *The Wanderground*, The Women's Press, London, 1985 edn

Gilman, Charlotte Perkins (1915), *Herland*, The Women's Press, London, 1979 edn

Hall, Radclyffe (1928), *The Well of Loneliness*, Virago, London, 1981 edn

Hart, Ellen (1992), *Stage Fright*, The Women's Press, London, 1994 edn

—(1994), *A Small Sacrifice*, The Women's Press, London, 1996 edn

—(1995), *Faint Praise*, The Women's Press, London, 1997 edn

—(1996), *Robber's Wine*, The Women's Press, London, 1997 edn

Kelly, Maggie, *Burning Issues*, Onlywomen Press, London, 1995

Kelly, Vivien, *Dirty Work*, Onlywomen Press, London, 1995

Livia, Anna, *Bulldozer Rising*, Onlywomen Press, London, 1987

—, 'Angel Alice', in Anna Livia and Lilian Mohin, eds, *The Pied Piper: Lesbian Feminist Fiction*, Onlywomen Press, London, 1989

McDermid, Val, *Report for Murder*, The Women's Press, London, 1987

—, *Common Murder*, The Women's Press, London, 1989

—, *Final Edition*, The Women's Press, London, 1991

—, *Dead Beat*, Victor Gollancz, London, 1992

—, *Kick Back*, Victor Gollancz, London, 1993

—, *Union Jack*, The Women's Press, London, 1993

—, *Crack Down*, HarperCollins, London, 1994

—, *Booked for Murder*, The Women's Press, London, 1996

—, *Clean Break*, HarperCollins, London, 1995

—, *Blue Genes*, HarperCollins, London, 1996

Maitland, Sara (1984), *Virgin Territory*, Pavanne, London, 1995 edn

—, *Three Times Table*, Chatto and Windus, London, 1990

—, *Home Truths*, Chatto and Windus, London, 1993

March, Caeia, *Three Ply Yarn*, The Women's Press, London, 1986

—, *The Hide and Seek Files*, The Women's Press, London, 1988

—, *Between the Worlds*, The Women's Press, London, 1996

Miller, Isabel (1969), *Patience and Sarah*, The Women's Press, London, 1979 edn

Miner, Valeric, *Murder in the English Department*, The Women's Press, London, 1982

Morgan, Claire (Patricia Highsmith), (1952), *The Price of Salt*, Naiad Press, Florida, 1984 edn

Namjoshi, Suniti, *Feminist Fables*, Sheba Feminist Publishers, London, 1981

—, *The Conversations of Cow*, The Women's Press, London, 1985

—, *The Blue Donkey Fables*, The Women's Press, London, 1988

—, 'Pelican' in Anna Livia and Lilian Mohin, eds, *The*

Pied Piper: Lesbian Feminist Fiction, Onlywomen Press, London, 1989

Piercy, Marge (1976), *Woman on the Edge of Time*, The Women's Press, London, 1979 edn

Russ, Joanna (1975), *The Female Man*, The Women's Press, London, 1985 edn

Sarton, May (1961), *The Small Room*, The Women's Press, London, 1996

—, *Mrs Stevens hears the mermaids singing*, Norton, New York, 1965; The Women's Press, London, 1993

—, *As We Are Now*, Norton, New York, 1973; The Women's Press, London, 1983

—, *A Reckoning*, Norton, New York, 1978; The Women's Press, London, 1984

—, *The Education of Harriet Hatfield*, Norton, New York, 1989; The Women's Press, London, 1990

Scott, Manda, *Hen's Teeth*, The Women's Press, London, 1996

Stanley, Julia Penelope and Susan J. Wolfe, *The Coming Out Stories*, Persephone Press, Watertown, Massachusetts, 1980

Toder, Nancy, *Choices*, Persephone Press, Watertown, Massachusetts, 1980

Wilson, Barbara, *Murder in the Collective*, The Women's Press, London, 1984

—(1986), *Sisters of the Road*, The Women's Press, London, 1987 edn

Wilson, Anna, *Altogether Elsewhere*, Onlywomen Press, London, 1985

Wings, Mary, *She Came Too Late*, The Women's Press, London, 1986

—, *She Came in a Flash*, The Women's Press, London, 1988

—, *Divine Victim*, The Women's Press, London, 1992

—, *She Came by the Book*, The Women's Press, London, 1995

—, *She Came to the Castro*, The Women's Press, London, 1997

Winterson, Jeanette (1985), *Oranges Are Not The Only*

Fruit, Vintage, London, 1991 edn
—(1990), *Written on the Body*, Jonathan Cape, London, 1992 edn
—, *Art & Lies*, Vintage, London, 1995
—, *Gut Symmetries*, Granta, London, 1997

Theoretical and Critical Works

Auchmuty, Rosemary, *A World of Girls*, The Women's Press, London, 1992

Coward, Rosalind, 'Are Women's Novels Feminist Novels?', in Elaine Showalter, ed, *The New Feminist Criticism: Essays on Women, Literature and Theory*, Pantheon Books, New York, 1985; Virago, London,1986

Daly, Mary (1978), *Gyn/Ecology: The Metaethics of Radical Feminism*, The Women's Press, London, 1979 edn

Duncker, Patricia, 'Writing and Roaring: In Search of the Truly Political Feminist Novel', *Trouble and Strife* 6 (Summer 1985)

—, *Sisters and Strangers: An Introduction to Contemporary Feminist Fiction*, Blackwell, Oxford, and Cambridge, Mass., 1992

Faderman, Lillian (1980), *Surpassing the Love of Men: Romantic Friendship and Love between Women from the Renaissance to the Present*, The Women's Press, London, 1985 edn

—, *Odd Girls and Twilight Lovers: A History of Lesbian Life in Twentieth-Century America*, Columbia University Press, New York, 1991; Penguin Books, Harmondsworth, 1992

Frye, Marilyn, *The Politics of Reality*, The Crossing Press, New York, 1983

Griffin, Gabriele, ed, *Outwrite: Lesbianism and Popular Culture*, Pluto Press, London and Boulder, Colorado, 1993

Harne, Lynne and Elaine Miller, eds, *All the Rage: Reasserting Radical Lesbian Feminism*, The Women's Press, London, 1996

Harne, Lynne and Rights of Women, *Valued Families: The Lesbian Mothers' Legal Handbook*, The Women's Press, London, 1997

Hobby, Elaine and Chris White, eds, *What Lesbians Do in Books*, The Women's Press, London, 1991

Jeffreys, Sheila (1993), *The Lesbian Heresy: A Feminist Perspective on the Lesbian Sexual Revolution*, The Women's Press, London, 1994 edn

—, *The Idea of Prostitution*, Spinifex Press, Melbourne, 1997

Kitzinger, Celia and Rachel Perkins, *Changing Our Minds: Lesbian Feminism and Psychology*, Onlywomen Press, London, 1993

Lesbian History Group, *Not a Passing Phase: Reclaiming Lesbians in History 1840–1985*, The Women's Press, London, 1989

The Lesbian Review of Books: An International Quarterly Review of Books by, for, and about Lesbians, 42 Wainaku Avenue, 206, Hilo, HI 96720, USA

Mason-John, Valerie, ed, *Talking Black: Lesbians of African and Asian Descent Speak Out*, Cassell, London, 1995

Mason-John, Valerie and Ann Khambatta, *Lesbians Talk: Making Black Waves*, Scarlet Press, London, 1993

Millett, Kate (1969), *Sexual Politics*, Abacus, London, 1972 edn

Munt, Sally, ed, *New Lesbian Criticism: Literary and Cultural Readings*, Harvester Wheatsheaf, Hemel Hempstead, 1992

—, *Murder by the Book? Feminism and the Crime Novel*, Routledge, London and New York, 1994

Palmer, Paulina, *Contemporary Women's Fiction: Narrative Practice and Feminist Theory*, Harvester Wheatsheaf, Hemel Hempstead, 1989

—, *Contemporary Lesbian Writing: Dreams, Desire, Difference*, Open University Press, Buckingham, 1993

Radford, Jill and Diana E. H. Russell, eds, *Femicide: The Politics of Woman Killing*, Twayne Publishers, New York, 1992

Raitt, Suzanne, ed, *Volcanoes and Pearl Divers: Essays in Lesbian Feminist Studies*, Onlywomen Press, London, 1995

Raymond, Janice, *A Passion for Friends: Towards a Philosophy of Female Affection*, The Women's Press, London, 1986

Reti, Irene, ed, *Unleashing Feminism: Critiquing Lesbian Sadomasochism in the Gay Nineties*, HerBooks, Santa Cruz, 1993

Rule, Jane, *Lesbian Images*, Peter Davies, London, 1976

Smith, Barbara, 'Towards a Black Feminist Criticism', in Elaine Showalter, ed, *The New Feminist Criticism: Essays on Women, Literature and Theory*, Pantheon Books, New York, 1985; Virago, London, 1986

Trouble and Strife: The Radical Feminist Magazine, PO Box 8, Diss, Norfolk IP22 3XG, UK

Walker, Alice (1983), *In Search of Our Mothers' Gardens: Womanist Prose*, The Women's Press, London, 1984

—, *Anything We Love Can Be Saved: A Writer's Activism*, The Women's Press, London, 1998

Wall, Cheryl A., ed, *Changing Our Own Words: Essays on Criticism, Theory and Writing by Black Women*, Routledge, London, 1990

Wittig, Monique (1980), *The Straight Mind*, Harvester Wheatsheaf, London, 1992 edn

Zimmerman, Bonnie, 'What Has Never Been: An Overview of Lesbian Feminist Criticism', in Elaine Showalter, ed, *The New Feminist Criticism: Essays on Women, Literature and Theory*, Pantheon Books, New York, 1985; Virago, London, 1986

—, *The Safe Sea of Women: Lesbian Fiction 1969–1989*, Beacon Press, Boston, 1990; Onlywomen Press, London, 1992

—, 'Lesbians Like This and That: Some Notes on Lesbian Criticism for the Nineties', in Sally Munt, ed, *New Lesbian Criticism: Literary and Cultural Readings*, Harvester Wheatsheaf, Hemel Hempstead, 1992

INDEX